DOLLHOUSE FURNITURE

DOLLHOUSE FURNITURE

Margaret Towner

COURAGE BOOKS

An Imprint of
RUNNING PRESS
Philadelphia, Pennsylvania

A QUINTET BOOK

Canadian Representatives:
General Publishing Co., Ltd.
30 Lesmill Road, Don Mills
Ontario M3B 2T6

9 8 7 6 5 4 3 2 1
Digit on the right indicates the number of this printing

Library of Congress
Cataloging-in-Publication Number
93–70595

ISBN 1–56138–325–2

This book was designed and produced by
Quintet Publishing Limited
6 Blundell Street
London N7 9BH

Creative Director: Richard Dewing
Senior Editor: Laura Sandelson
Designer: James Lawrence
Editor: Alison Leach
Photographer: Nick Nicholson

Typeset in Great Britain by
Central Southern Typesetters, Eastbourne
Manufactured in Singapore by Colour Trend Pte Ltd
Printed in Hong Kong by Leefung-Asco Printers Ltd

AUTHOR ACKNOWLEDGEMENTS

I would like to thank most sincerely all those friends who have
generously helped with the preparation of this book. Among others
these include: Olivia Bristol, Kay Desmonde, Jane Dunn, Peter and
Joan Dunk, Liza Dunluce, Nick and Esther Forder, Joan Gibson,
Vivien Greene, Flora Gill Jacobs, Christine Jeffreys, Gillian
Kernon, Marjorie McCann, Marion Osborne and June Stowe.
Thanks are also due to all the correspondents of *International Dolls'
House News* over the last 25 years who have shared their knowledge
of the subject, and who have given me untold pleasure and
information.

The Publishers would like to thank *The Singing Tree*, London SW6,
for allowing their miniature furniture to be photographed for Chapter 6.

Published by Courage Books
an imprint of Running Press Book Publishers
125 South Twenty-second Street
Philadelphia, Pennsylvania 19103–4399

CONTENTS

AN INTRODUCTION TO DOLLHOUSES AND THEIR CONTENTS

CHAPTER

1

ABOVE **A Stockbroker Tudor house by Triang, 1930s.**

LEFT **Overall view of the earliest true dollhouse, dated 1611, in the Germanisches Nationalmuseum, Nuremberg, Germany.**

Miniature objects have given people pleasure throughout history. The creation of such images has long been a part of most arts and crafts. At all times of peace and prosperity, a craftsman could probably be found in the back streets of any town, making small models of people and of their houses and other possessions.

The uses made of these models do, of course, vary in different cultures. Sometimes they are religious objects or are intended to provide magical help in the afterworld. Sometimes they are curiosities or, when made in precious materials, symbols of wealth. Sometimes they are made as technical aids for an architect or salesman. Sometimes they are toys for children, to use in games that mimic adult life.

Dollhouses and their furniture have been included in most of these categories at different times, and today collectors are more numerous than ever before. Twenty years ago, an adult interest in dollhouses was considered eccentric, but such an interest, even sometimes amounting to a passion, is not new, as a look at the history of the subject will show. Various reasons for this attachment to miniature objects could be suggested.

The collector of toy soldiers is perhaps a closet Napoleon, seeking to control the fates of his helpless armies. Not many dollhouse collectors have a similar wish to dominate; it is more likely that they are trying to recreate the image of a happy and secure home environment in miniature. Whatever the underlying motives, the collector will obtain a great deal of pleasure in searching for, restoring, and arranging the contents of a dollhouse and, incidentally, is almost certain to acquire a better understanding and knowledge of the home life of former generations.

The aim of this book is to introduce the reader to the immense range of furniture that has been made for dollhouses. In a museum or a private collection, such furniture is rarely seen on its own but is usually part of the carefully chosen contents of a dollhouse, the impact of the complete arrangement being much greater than the isolated elements. Furniture on its own tends to look like the sad contents of an auction room: its setting is all important.

Finding an interesting dollhouse that will be rewarding to furnish is the best way to start a collection. This first chapter therefore sets the scene with a brief account of dollhouses up to the present time, the reasons they were made, who made them, and how the original owners acquired their contents.

Early Model Houses
~

What is almost certainly the earliest dollhouse is a clay model made in an agricultural community near Kiev, in the Ukraine, in the third millenium BC. The people lived quietly, and women appear to have played an important part in the community. The model shows a circular hut, raised on wooden piles, which would have had a thatched roof. Inside the porch a woman is grinding corn, and beside her are three storage jars on a shelf. In the middle of the hut is a low table, and by the wall is a large stove, beside which another woman is sitting. Model buildings were made in many ancient civilizations, including Egypt, but most are not a clear celebration of domestic life, as this one was.

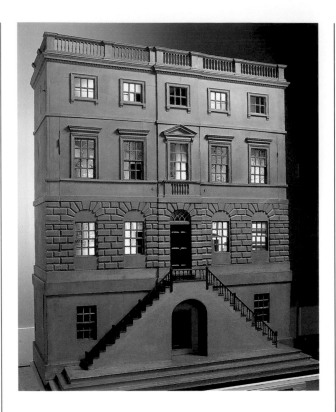

ABOVE **Overall view of the mid-18th century Blackett baby house in the Museum of London.**

Another early model house was made for the funeral of a lady of the Roman Empire, who was living in Holland in the 2nd century AD. The inside of her rectangular stone casket is carved in high relief as a model room, with a cushioned armchair, a cupboard with paneled doors, cosmetics and other items on a three-tiered shelf unit, a three-legged table with lions' heads, and the lady herself reclining on a comfortable cushioned couch in the attitude of Madame Récamier. After this glimpse of civilized life, the dollhouse disappeared into the Dark Ages, and was not heard of again for another 1,400 years.

Model houses, where the furniture is fixed permanently in place, are not really satisfactory, either as children's toys or for adult collectors, as they are static, giving no scope for the owners to exercise their imaginations or enjoy moving the contents around. Part of the pleasure of a real dollhouse is being able to add to, or rearrange, the furnishings. The owner can devise a multitude of social occasions for the inhabitants of the dollhouse, weddings and Christmas being especially popular. Dollhouses tend to be passed on from generation to generation, and each new owner likes to alter the contents to suit her personal taste.

Models are nevertheless very attractive, and, because they are not subject to change, provide a glimpse of domestic life in the past. For these reasons they are still made and collected. Decorative model furniture can be constructed of relatively fragile materials, such as paper, card or cork, as the houses are usually protected by fixed glass.

Pride of Possession
~

The true dollhouse appeared quite suddenly, in wonderful detail and completeness, in southern Germany in the early 17th century. The important trading cities of Augsberg, Nuremberg, and Munich were centers of prosperity and skill. Despite intermittent wars, life in the great households of the nobles and wealthy merchants had developed to a state of luxury and complexity. A study of one of their miniature houses shows that not only was the family provided with the latest fashion in ornate and luxurious furniture, but that immense pride was also taken in having suitable equipment for every domestic task.

It was this pride of possession that certainly inspired the construction of these houses, which have an affinity with the cabinets of *objets d'art* also popular at the time. The earliest surviving houses in the Germanisches Nationalmuseum in Nuremberg, Germany, are dated 1611 and 1639. A characteristic of these houses is that the exteriors are relatively elaborate architecturally, like a real house, rather than a piece of furniture. Similarly, the interiors are structured like a house, with staircases and landings, rather than being just a collection of room boxes.

Such attention to detail is far from common in houses of later periods, and is indicative of the attitude of the owners, who expected a response of admiration and envy from those invited to view. And, of course, this is still the response of visitors to the museum.

These collectors would not have bought ready-made houses or furniture; they would probably have commissioned an artist to draw up plans to their satisfaction, and he would have had the house and its contents made by individual craftsmen, such as cabinet makers, metalworkers, and glassmakers. The kitchen was as highly regarded as it is in homes today, and was given a prominent position and elaborate treatment, with every possible implement correctly made and in its place.

Smaller dollhouses were made, such as one in London's Bethnal Green Museum, where the entire ground floor consists of a double kitchen, one for displaying dishes and eating, and one for cooking. The successor to this type of layout was the simple Nuremberg toy kitchen, seen as an educational aid to teach young girls how to recognize and use the various pieces of equipment. It was equipped for children to cook, and was therefore usually made to a larger scale than most dollhouses. It continued to be a feature of German homes throughout the next three centuries.

Towards the end of the 17th century, grand houses were also made in Holland for wealthy Dutch families whose motives were similar to those of the German merchants. The houses tended to be far less architectural. They are mostly rooms grouped in a large cabinet, rather than in a house.

ABOVE **Exterior of the King's Lynn baby house, British, c.1740, notable for its fine proportions** and craftsmanship that are typical of the first half of the 18th century.

They often contain mural paintings and porcelain of high quality, and they are peopled with fine wax dolls in the formal costumes and wigs of the period. Houses continued to be made in this tradition in Holland throughout the 18th century. A number of them can be seen in museums in Amsterdam, The Hague, and Utrecht.

Also in the 18th century, the British developed a tradition of "baby" houses ("baby" then being the word for doll). Since the English monarchs William and Mary came from Holland, and the next dynasty of rulers was from Germany, Britain had close links with these countries at this period. The earlier surviving houses show this influence, and there are some cabinet houses. The British, however, mostly preferred the idea of a real house, and this was to become the norm. At this time the building of country houses, with their landscaped gardens, was absorbing much energy and wealth in Britain. Baby houses never seem to have become quite such an obsession with the British, whose domestic way of life was much simpler compared with the Continental style.

The houses are, therefore, less elaborate, sometimes perhaps designed by an architect but assembled by an estate carpenter. While some, such as the one at Nostell Priory, in the county of Yorkshire in northern England, have fine staircases and paneling, others soon started to appear whose detail is confined to elegant façades, or which are small and simple, like the little house at Norwich Museum, Norfolk, to the northeast of London. Rather than being showpieces, they became a special kind of children's toy. The earliest American house, the Van Cortlandt Manor, New York, dated 1744–1774 on the front, is of this modest and attractive kind.

Houses from the Georgian period (18th and early 19th century) are the earliest likely to become available to the collector, mainly at auction sales, but they are, of course, very expensive, particularly if they have original furniture. The collector of dollhouse furniture needs to think hard before buying a large, empty house of this period: it will be almost impossible to find contemporary furniture, and because scale was not then standardized in any way, furniture of a later period may well look too small and insignificant.

Early 19th-century houses continued to be made in both Britain and America as one-off commissions for individual families. Often very solidly made, they tended at first to have purpose-made stands. Later on, especially in America, they became increasingly elaborate, reflecting the growing wealth

RIGHT **The interior of a large turn-of-the-century mansion, fully furnished with the abundance of objects available then. (*Courtesy of Christie's, London.*)**

BELOW RIGHT **An unusual box-back house with Gothic façade; the interior has four plain rooms.**

BELOW **A typical British box-back house, with brick above and stucco below.**

of the time, and the romantic styles of Victorian architecture. Middle-class families in America became involved in building houses for their children as a hobby, and some very fanciful edifices were produced. All these houses are now very sought after by collectors.

First Commercial Dollhouses

The late 18th century saw the beginning of the commercial dollhouse as a regular article of trade, both in Britain and in Germany. In Britain, the early dollhouses were usually

constructed in a simple box, divided into two, four or more rooms, often without a staircase. Architectural detail was confined to the front, which was usually hinged as a single cupboard door. This door generally projects at the top above the box at the back, in the manner of a Georgian terrace (or row) house in London, where the gutters and chimneys are hidden by the cornice. Usually the dollhouse roof is flat, but sometimes it is pitched.

Once known as Silber & Fleming houses, from the name of a well-known wholesaler that included them in its catalog, they were made by small London workshops, in slightly varying styles and widely different qualities, from the late 18th century to the early 20th century. They are also known as box-backs. In buying a house of this type, the collector needs to study the proportions of the rooms, which in some later examples can be very cramped, mean-looking, and difficult to furnish.

In Germany, the doll's kitchen continued to be popular, and doll's rooms developed on the same principle of a three-sided box open at the top and front, either single or grouped in twos and threes side by side. These are shown in the 1800 catalogue of Bestelmeier, a Nuremberg toy merchant, and they became a regular product of 19th-century firms in Saxony and elsewhere.

It is said that they were more popular than actual houses because they fitted into the small urban dwellings of the middle-class families in Germany, but it is more likely that they are simply a traditional shape. Because they cannot be

ABOVE **A small, rococo-style open room, with the original curtains, labelled by the Danish** **retailer, Thorngreen of Copenhagen. (*Courtesy of Christie's, London.*)**

closed, they are easily damaged and become dusty. They have never been popular in Britain or America, so they were not exported there, but they have retained a hold in Germany, Switzerland, and France. They are ideal for display, and many of them can be seen in European museums.

ABOVE **German open rooms c.1909, elegantly furnished and owing much to their attractive** **contemporary wallpapers. (*Courtesy of Christie's, London.*)**

ABOVE **A large, late-Victorian house, front-opening, wide and fairly shallow, making it ideal for displaying furniture.**

Early Developments

~

Being heavy in comparison with most toys, dollhouses were expensive to transport, and they did not form a significant part of the export trade of the German toy industry until late in the 19th century. At this time color lithography became widely used on toys, and a lightweight type of dollhouse was developed on which highly decorative architectural detail could be expressed by printed papers. The principal factory involved is thought to be that of Moritz Gottschalk of Marienburg, Saxony, founded in 1865, since a sequence of styles and numerical marks has been traced linking these houses with later models (first identified by the author in a manufacturer's advertisement).

Known as "blue roofs," from the typical distemper color used to represent slates, they were made in an enormous number of sizes and variations, based on the decorative villa architecture of Germany and Austria. The smallest sometimes have all details, including windows and doors, printed on. The interiors are also elaborately decorated with specially printed wallpapers and floorpapers, and features such as metal door handles in a butterfly shape and cut-out balustrades in a pattern of linked circles frequently occur. The most expensive models have a profusion of turned and fretwork architectural detail, but they are usually very simple inside. Their decorative appeal makes all sizes very popular with collectors, but the smaller houses do not give much scope for furniture.

The later Gottschalk houses usually have red roofs, and these continued to be made until World War II. Similar houses were made by the firm of D. H. Wagner & Sohne of Grunhainichen, Germany, and other manufacturers. In America, R. Bliss Manufacturing Co. also specialized in paper-lithographed wooden toys, and for several decades

BELOW **A blue roof house, lithographed paper on wood, missing the lower balustrade and steps, probably by Moritz Gottschalk.**

BELOW **A small lithographed house, in the so-called Deauville type, early 20th century, manufacturer unknown.**

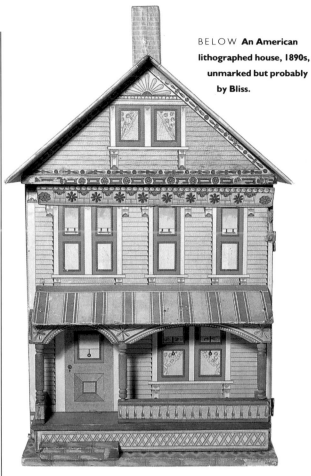

BELOW **An American lithographed house, 1890s, unmarked but probably by Bliss.**

from the 1880s produced a series of houses with many similarities to the blue roof type, which fortunately are very often marked "R. Bliss." Among others, the well-known toy firm of Albert Schoenhut also made a series of simpler houses and bungalows with lithographed decoration.

In Germany, also in the 1880s, a Nuremberg toy-maker, Christian Hacker, manufactured a range of much more solid houses. These were often constructed in horizontal sections for easy movement, and originally were usually flat-fronted with some lithographed decorations. The designs became much more varied in the early 1900s, some being of a continental villa style, with gardens, mansard roofs and outside blinds, and some like an old German town house. Others were based on London's suburban villas. Exported to most countries their origin is often mistaken, but they can sometimes be identified by a trademark on the base. These are also much sought after.

BELOW **The interior of the American lithographed house (above), its bright decor needing little furniture.**

BELOW **One of a variety of houses made by Christian Hacker in the early 1900s, No. 470/1, with the original decor.**

Other well-proportioned houses were made from about 1898 by the London firm of G. & J. Lines. These varied from simple cottages to large Edwardian (early 19th-century) mansions, and they were also exported. They are particularly handsome if they still have their original papered brick exteriors and colorful wallpapers. After World War I, the three sons of Joseph Lines set up a new business, in competition with their father, making houses that became known by their tradename of "Tri-ang." Between the wars they were especially known for their well-made Tudor-style houses, and for the copy of Princess Elizabeth's Welsh cottage. Lines was dominant over other firms at this time.

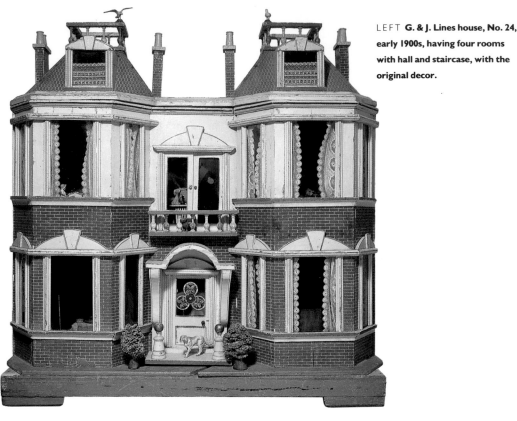

LEFT **G. & J. Lines house, No. 24, early 1900s, having four rooms with hall and staircase, with the original decor.**

Buying a Dollhouse

~

If you are intending to buy a house, either commercially manufactured or homemade, of the traditional type produced up to about 1939, mainly for the pleasure of collecting and displaying suitable furniture in it, there are several points to consider. Houses look best when they are furnished with either contemporary pieces or slightly later ones. Victorian furniture has now become quite expensive to collect, but it was manufactured in a wide range of scales, from the tiny sets which suit the smallest Gottschalk house to 1:12 or larger. Between the wars there was much less choice as to scale, but furniture and houses tended to become smaller.

Apart from scale, there is also the question of the proportions of the rooms. If the height of the ceilings and the size of doors and fireplaces demand a particular size of furniture, but the floor area is insufficient for a complete suite to be displayed without crowding, the house will be a problem. Staircases and landings provide a sense of realism and extra space for objects. A bathroom cannot usually be expected before the end of the 19th century, but it is a pleasure to furnish.

If space is limited and small houses are preferred, then some internal details will need to be sacrificed. Otherwise the woodwork in doors, baseboards, dados, cornices, and so on should be good quality. It is also of great importance that the house should have its original paintwork and wallpapers, as these are what give a real period background; collectors are prepared to pay a premium for houses in this condition, even if they seem rather worn.

Houses that open at the back are generally unpopular. Unless a turntable can be provided, the façade of the house must face the wall if the rooms are to be exposed. Even more difficult are bungalows designed to be seen from above by removal of the roof, which is inconvenient and unrealistic.

Recent Developments

~

The period since 1945 has seen significant changes in dollhouses. Material shortages postwar resulted in a gradual decrease in the amount of wood being used, and increased use of fiberboard, metal, and plastic. In America and Britain, a variety of lithographed steel houses made by firms such as Louis Marx, T. Cohn and Mettoy were successful, often taking furniture of less than 1:16. Plastic windows, doors, and roofs became common, and all-plastic houses began to appear, for example Jenny's Home by Tri-ang in the style of the modernist postwar housing of the 1960s. Inexpensive plastic houses imported from the Far East brought ready-furnished dollhouses within the reach of most children. Houses of the immediate postwar period reflect the homes created in the building boom of the time, and are well worth collecting, especially as a good variety of furniture was made for them, which is available at a reasonable price.

However, the popularity of a toy associated with a domestic life that was of increasingly less importance to the child diminished. The dollhouse might soon have almost disappeared, had it not been for the renewed interest of adults. This started in America, as the creative hobby of enthusiasts for scale miniature houses, and has since spread to Europe, especially Britain.

The emphasis on accuracy of scale and fine detail removes this activity from the realm of toy collecting, and has far more in common with the early German and Dutch miniature interiors. The major difference is that nowadays the houses are nearly always modeled on those of an earlier time, the aim being to recreate the past, rather than to celebrate the present. The quality of many of the miniature houses, especially those commissioned from artist/craftsmen such as the legendary Jim Marcus in America or David West in Britain, is, however, unsurpassed.

At more or less the same time, interest in the old dollhouses as a serious subject for the social and art historian was aroused, in particular by the researches of Vivien Greene and Flora Gill Jacobs. People started to collect these forgotten toys and to discover their history. Even now, far less detailed knowledge is available on dollhouses and their furniture than on any other aspect of toy or doll collecting; it is hoped that this book may be helpful to the novice and the experienced collector alike.

RIGHT **A Louis Marx lithographed tin plate house, showing detailed interior.**

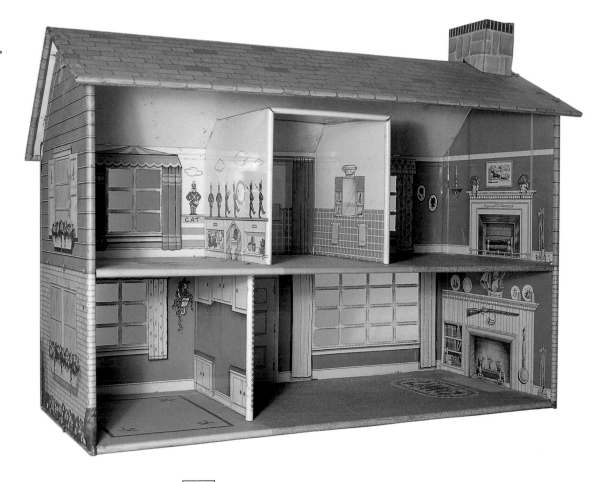

FURNITURE FROM THE 17TH TO THE EARLY 19TH CENTURIES

CHAPTER 2

ABOVE **Typical Rock & Graner**
pieces, with pierced galleries on
the *etagère* and sideboard, and
enameled upholstery.

The miniature furniture in the early German and Dutch dollhouses of the 17th and early 18th centuries is certainly the most beautiful ever made. Photographs of it in its original settings recall the Dutch paintings of interiors of the period, with their harmony of color and form. Every major dollhouse of this kind is, of course, in a museum, and the collector can only be pleased that they have been kept complete and have not been broken up for sale. Since this furniture cannot be "collected," except in pictures, only one example is given here.

The furniture in the dollhouse first owned by Petronella de la Court in the last quarter of the 17th century and now in the Centraal Museum, Utrecht, The Netherlands, is of the highest quality, and one can especially admire the barley sugar spiral turning of tables and chairs, then extremely fashionable. Nevertheless, realistic distinctions are kept between the highest quality pieces in the reception rooms and the sturdy, slightly rustic chairs and cupboards that can be seen in the kitchen.

Because the owners were able to call on craftsmen in every field in Amsterdam, the variety of materials used in the furnishings gives an impression of great liveliness. The kitchen has equipment in glass, silver, pottery, and porcelain. Elsewhere in the house are examples of miniature basketry, bookbinding, gilding, carving, and other domestic crafts.

LEFT **Ivory globes from Petronella de la Court's late 17th-century cabinet house, Utrecht, The Netherlands. (*Courtesy of Centraal Museum, Utrecht.*)**

ABOVE **Miniature British and Dutch silver, including a teapot, a chamber candlestick, snuffers, and a pair of tea caddies, first half of 18th century. (*Courtesy of Donohoe, London.*)**

On rare occasions, items intended for early European dollhouses do appear for sale. Being works of art in their own right, they are not usually sold as dollhouse fittings, but by specialists in various types of antiques. Miniature silver of the 17th and early 18th centuries was made by known craftsmen, including, among many others, Christiaen Waerenberg, Jan Breda and Arnoldus van Geffen in Holland, George Manjoy, David Clayton and John Hugh Le Sage in London, and John Coney in Boston. Examples of this work is available from silver specialists.

RIGHT **A silver-mounted, shagreen-cased canteen of miniature flatware, British or Dutch, c.1740. (*Courtesy of Donohoe, London.*)**

LEFT **Marble tables supported by carved gilt eagles, also from Petronella de la Court's cabinet house, Utrecht. (*Courtesy of Centraal Museum, Utrecht.*)**

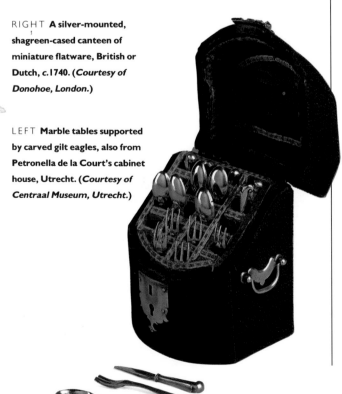

Miniature pewter objects of the same period were also made in large quantities in Britain and Germany from the 16th century onwards. Pieces dredged from rivers or found in archaeological digs can be obtained from time to time in Europe. These were made by craftsmen called "triflers," from the name of the alloy they used. Dishes and plates are by far the most common, sometimes with a Tudor rose embossed, but other items, such as miniature firebacks and pans, can also be found. Miniature porcelain items, made in China for export to Europe, were used for the china cabinets of dollhouses. The Christie's auction of salvage from the wreck of the *Vung Tau* cargo ship included vast numbers of little blue and white vases of this kind.

British Baby House Furniture
~

British baby house furniture of the 18th century bears no comparison with the Dutch, except in its sparing use of miniature silver, pewter, and brass ware of fine quality. Very few dollhouses have not been added to, or had replacement furniture in the last two centuries. One reason for this is that they were mostly quite sparsely furnished originally, with

ABOVE **A detail of bed from the mid-18th century Blackett baby house, showing construction and carefully made bedclothes. (*1992 Comstock/Julian Nieman/SGC.*)**

BELOW **The dining room of the Blackett baby house, showing the flat detailing of chairs and the fine silver. (*1992 Comstock/Julian Nieman/SGC.*)**

plain pieces. The effect, without later additions, would have been a little like the pictures of Georgian interiors by Arthur Devis, in which the owners sit proudly on a pair of chairs in an empty room.

Interest was provided by the use of textiles for bed-hangings, upholstery, and curtains. A precise scale was not followed, but the rooms often take furniture of up to 1:6.

A baby house reputed to have belonged to the daughters of King George III contains a set of painted Adam-style wheelback chairs in this size, which, not surprisingly, are better made than most. The usual complement was very simple tables and chairs, with the detail of backs and legs only suggested in two dimensions, chests of drawers, toilet mirrors, corner cupboards and cradles, although occasionally high-quality miniature cabinet pieces are found.

It is perhaps appropriate here to touch on the knotty problem of the difference between cabinet pieces, salesman's samples, apprentice pieces, and dollhouse furniture. My opinion is that the salesman's sample can be authenticated as such only if it shows a number of alternative shapings on the same piece. The apprentice piece, if indeed it exists in miniature form, would have had to be constructed exactly like the best kind of 18th-century cabinet work, or it could not have qualified the apprentice to make full-sized furniture.

The miniature chest or bureau with fine craftsmanship, which is usually larger than dollhouse size, was made, as it is sometimes today, as a pretty receptacle for jewelry or other odds and ends. Simple furniture, usually chairs and tables, was made in a middling size to cope with doll's tea parties, as shown in a charming painting by Hogarth in Cardiff Museum, Wales. Similar but smaller furniture was made, also quite simply, for the baby house.

In the 18th century, shops such as Deards in the Haymarket, Coles Child on Old London Bridge, and Bellamy in Holborn were already in existence, supplying, among other trifles, commercial fittings for the baby house. In America a firm called Adrian Forst of Philadelphia was selling similar pieces in 1817. A bill among the household accounts at Temple Newsam near Leeds, Yorkshire, in northern England, detailing toys purchased by Lord Irwin for his five little daughters, includes:

1 pair of Chest of Drawers	*6 shillings*
1 Toy Bureau	*6 shillings*
1 dozen of Gilt Dishes	*2 shillings*
1 dozen of Plates	*six pence*

ABOVE **A detail of the Blackett baby house kitchen, showing a working brass model spit and grate. (*1992 Comstock/Julian Nieman/SGC.*)**

RIGHT **Late 18th-century printed Staffordshire pottery, from the kitchen of the Norwich baby house.**

ABOVE **A set of 18th-century
brass grates, for a parlor, a
kitchen, and a dining room.**

Among other goods available at shops were upholstered
furniture, kitchen equipment, and brass and steel grates for
the fireplace. Sets of brass grates, carefully styled for the
drawing room, bedroom and kitchen, are still found
regularly, although in very grand houses such as Nostell
Priory, Yorkshire, such objects may have been specially
made. Brass warming pans, fire irons, candle snuffers, and
plate holders were all made commercially. The original
pieces of this period are much heavier for their size and more
neatly made than later reproductions. All these items are now
extremely rare.

Even less common are the miniature dinner and tea
services made in British Worcester or Caughley soft-paste
porcelain. Such toy services were usually made in a doll's
size, and were only occasionally small enough for the baby
house. Staffordshire pottery pieces are slightly less rare, the
blue and white transfer-printed wares being especially
charming. Creamware, made by Wedgwood and Leeds
factories in Britain, was also used for miniature sets, which
had delightful modeled food on the plates.

Early Types

Apart from the silverware, which because of the marking
systems can usually be traced to a maker, and the better
known ceramics, virtually all 18th-century items are
anonymous, although they sometimes bear a shop label.
Collectors must rely on a knowledge of full-sized antique
pieces to establish age and origin. It should, however, be
borne in mind that dollhouse furniture, unlike larger pieces,
has not been subject to 200 years of hard wear, since dolls do
not scuff their chairs or spill beer on tables! The furniture
can, therefore, seem alarmingly new-looking, especially if
unpolished for long periods.

Anonymity only starts to break down early in the 19th
century, when the dollhouse had entirely ceased to be an
adult amusement. Manufacturers were ready to supply a
rising middle class with inexpensive toys for the children.
George Bestelmeier of Nuremberg, Germany, was already
exporting sets of wooden and metal furniture in 1800, as his
catalog shows.

The earliest types of German furniture commonly found in
several scales are of unpainted wood, packed in sets in oval
wooden boxes. The styles are simple, based on those of the
Empire period but showing their provincial origin in the
remote hilly areas of the Erzgebirge and Thuringia.
Decoration is usually confined to small inlays of contrasting
wood. A similar type is painted red, with a typical small inlay
on the centers of tables, and a diamond-shaped piece of
leather decorating the struts of the seat-backs.

Once a type of furniture was in production in Germany, it
continued to be made for many decades after the style

LEFT **Part of a Wedgwood
creamware dinner service, with a
modeled chicken, leg of lamb, and
vegetables. This high-quality
pottery, copying silver shapes,
was in general use from 1770
onwards.**

RIGHT **A mirror, cabinet, and wardrobe with a shallow tray on top, the wood grained to imitate walnut. German, 1840s.**

LEFT **Part of a set of inlaid wood furniture: a chair, a chest of drawers with a sewing box on top (note the fixed pincushion), and a fall-front secretaire. German, early 19th century.**

became unfashionable; usually a deterioration is evident in the workmanship of later pieces. The furniture was traded by agents, who produced magnificent catalogs, with the illustrations colored by hand.

A number of these catalogs survive; the Sonneberg Toy Catalogue of 1831 shows sets of plain wooden furniture with bone and inlay decoration, and painted pieces decorated with flowers. The red-painted furniture was made in Saxony, and appears in a catalog of 1850. In the same areas, sets of tea, dinner, toilet and kitchen utensils were turned in lime wood, as a very satisfactory substitute for china, and were also packed in oval boxes.

LEFT **Early Empire-style, red-painted wood furniture. Saxony, from 1830 onwards.**

Some British Makers

~

After the Napoleonic wars toys were sold in British shops and bazaars, such as the Soho Bazaar which opened in 1816. Until recently little was known about the makers, but two major British manufacturers have been traced through my research. The first, John Bubb, had a workshop in Long Lane, Southwark, London. He made furniture in mahogany in the traditional Georgian styles, which continued to be produced for unfashionable homes until the middle of the 19th century. The pieces include round, tilt-top pedestal tables, flap dining tables, bureaus and glazed cabinets, which are marked "J Bubb. Maker" with an impressed stamp. John Bubb was in business, describing himself as a toymaker and dealer, between 1809 and about 1837, and an insurance policy shows he must have had a substantial turnover, his stock in 1809 being valued at £120 ($216).

Pieces of his are often found in large-scale dollhouses of this period, together with unmarked furniture of similar character, and these are occasionally found available for

sale. Bubb also made doll-sized pieces in similar styles. The quality of his furniture is not outstanding, but it is strongly made and very elegant. The wood used is lightweight, and the brass escutcheons on chests are purely decorative, as there are no locks. Bubb epitomizes the successful toymaker who makes no pretence of producing gems of Georgian cabinet work.

An even more successful British business was Evans & Cartwright of Dudley Road, Wolverhampton, in the English Midlands. This firm, whose furniture was once known as Orley and thought to be French or German, has been positively identified from the name, which is impressed, rather indistinctly, on some chairs.

BELOW **A chest, dining table, and tilt-top table by John Bubb. 1810–40.**

ABOVE **The underside of the tilt-top table shown left, showing his impressed mark, J. Bubb. Maker.**

LEFT **An Evans & Cartwright cast metal and tinplate mock-bamboo armchair and side chairs, enameled yellow with floral decoration, c.1825–30.**

SIDNEY CARTWRIGHT

John Evans of Wolverhampton, Britain, started the business in the first decade of the 19th century. He married a widow called Mrs. Cartwright, and took his stepson Sidney into the firm.

The boy's aptitude must have become evident very quickly, for by the age of 14 he was acting as the firm's traveler. He was soon taken into partnership, and, being an able businessman with considerable financial acumen, set about expanding the business, which became the only important firm making tin toys in Britain. Sidney, whose portrait shows him to have had aspirations to a fashionably romantic appearance, was later involved in banking and mining ventures. He was soon a magistrate and a pillar of local society. He married, but had no children. He and his wife left their collection of paintings, many of them showing Victorian family interiors, to the local art gallery. Sidney died a wealthy man in 1882.

ABOVE **Sidney Cartwright, a successful maker of tin plate and other dollhouse furniture during** the 19th century. (*Courtesy of Wolverhampton Art Gallery.*)

In the early 19th century Wolverhampton was the center of the British tinplate trade, making and exporting both plain domestic articles and decorative stove-enameled trays and so forth. Evans & Cartwright made simple tin toys that were sold at fairs (the factory became known locally as Whistle Hall), and decorative enameled toy furniture. The earliest examples of the latter were probably the mock-bamboo Chinese chairs with seats in pressed tinplate and cast pewter legs and backs, which are Regency (early 19th-century) in style.

A set of these attractive chairs, painted yellow with floral decoration, survives in Queen Victoria's childhood dollhouse at Kensington Palace, London. Other chairs, in a variety of styles of cast metal back and in a dark brown finish, sometimes with yellow, blue and green decorative touches, are of a similar period.

The firm's most popular line, however, was definitely the range made in tinplate painted in an orange-brown mottled imitation mahogany in the style of William IV. These pieces include dining chairs with two types of crest rail, hall chairs,

BELOW **An Evans & Cartwright washstand (jug and basin not original) and black and gilt tinplate fireplace. A Waltershausen clock with bone pillars and two Chinese porcelain vases.**

RIGHT **Evans & Cartwright pressed tinplate chairs, pedestal and console tables, and sofa, with a streaky yellow/brown japanned finish, the black seats imitating horsehair. 1830–1850.**

two types of sofa, console tables, a worktable, round and oval pedestal tables, a three-legged table, a wardrobe, washstands with pewter jug and basin, a longcase and a table clock, and a cradle. Fireplaces and kitchen ranges were made in black and gilt tinplate and there is also a simple, rush-seated kitchen chair.

This furniture, which was made up at least to 1850 and was exported, attracted the attention of Charles Dickens. He refers to it in his story *The Christmas Tree* as being "wonderfully made in Wolverhampton." The importance of this factory, which was producing highly finished tin toys as early or earlier than the better known German firms of Staudt, Märklin and Rock & Graner, has yet to be widely recognized.

RIGHT **Waltershausen (Schneegas) imitation rosewood chairs and ladies' toilet table with integral sewing drawer. Gothic style, 1840–50.**

Some German Makers

Meanwhile in Germany a firm in Thuringia had begun to make a range of furniture that was to supply dollhouses in Europe and America for nearly a century. The firm of Schneegas, later to become Gebrüder Schneegas und Sohne,

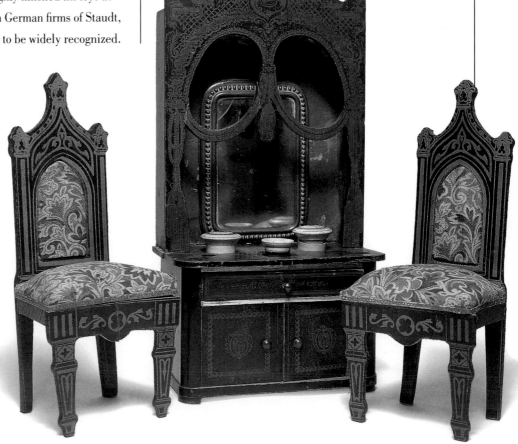

LEFT **A Waltershausen kneehole dressing table with mirror and writing desk, in mixed Louis/ Gothic style, imitation rosewood with transfer gilt decoration.**

was identified as the maker of this furniture in 1962 by Vivien Greene as a result of pioneering research in the East German town of Waltershausen. As it is easily recognizable, well-made, supplied in an infinite range of models, elegant and almost indestructible, it is avidly collected.

Founded in the 1840s, the firm first started production in the style known as Biedermeier, combining simple lines with restrained decoration of ivory, which had spread from Austria through Germany and eastern Europe. The earliest pieces are of very high quality. The wood used is almost without grain, does not shrink and is light in color, the surface being skillfully treated to resemble rosewood.

Other styles followed, mostly having gilt transfer decorations to imitate buhl inlay. A revived Gothic style is relatively rare, a Victorian revived rococo with curved outlines being more usual. Another, quite uncommon variety with actual metal mounts, also in the mid-century, was the Louis rococo style. However, it seems that once a model had been made, this stayed in production alongside newer pieces, so that it is possible to find a Biedermeier secretaire or a late Empire chair in the much inferior quality associated with the end of the century or later. Upholstery is usually in plain silk – purple, green, or blue – but sometimes a patterned cotton is used. The edges of the upholstery are trimmed with narrow gilt paper impressed with a beaded pattern.

FAR LEFT **The top of a Waltershausen table, showing two buildings in a hilly area, captioned "Inselberg" – a rare souvenir piece, from a mountain resort near Waltershausen.**

LEFT **A mid-19th century Waltershausen Biedermeier sofa and cabinet, with gilt transfer decoration.**

It would be interesting to list the whole range of pieces made by this firm, but this would be a herculean task, as there must be several hundred, some made in up to five different scales. However, the most rare and delightful pieces include an embroidery frame complete with canvas, and the bachelor's bed that folds away into a cupboard. It is to be hoped that the previously mentioned Mrs. Greene's study of this firm's catalogs will be published some day.

Similar furniture in the Biedermeier style was made in a blonde wood to imitate birch or satinwood, probably by the same firm, in lesser quantities. It is not as sought-after as

rosewood furniture, but in fact, when arranged in a room, has a much less gloomy effect than the dark wood finish. Another type, probably made by a different firm as it is slightly cruder in construction, has a hand-grained dark finish, perhaps representing walnut. This furniture was shown in an 1840 catalog auctioned by Sotheby's in 1991, so it is contemporary with the earlier Waltershausen, but considering its age and quality has been somewhat neglected.

RIGHT **Two different Waltershausen Louis-style dressing tables, both rosewood with metal mounts, showing the great variety of designs produced.**

LEFT **A Rock & Graner bed, with elegant fretted tinplate, hand-grained as mahogany.**

RIGHT **A Rock & Graner bedroom, showing typical serpent supports to the washstand and yellow painted linings.**

The firm of Rock & Graner from Biberach, Württemberg, made metal toys of all kinds in Germany from about 1813. Research by Baecker and Vaterlein has established its standing in the mid-century, when it exhibited at the 1851 Crystal Palace Exhibition, London, and many other fairs, its continuance and gradual decline towards the latter end of the century, and its sale to one Oskar Egelhaaf in 1896. The firm was eventually closed between 1904 and 1906.

The earliest Rock & Graner furniture styles are in a revived rococo and seem to date from the 1840s. Like Evans & Cartwright, the company used pressed tinplate, hand-painted in a mottled brown to imitate wood, although the color is much darker. Upholstery is sometimes enameled on, sometimes in silk with gold buttoning; there are also easy chairs of the kind the French call "toads," with the metal frame upholstered all over. Very typical of the more decorative pieces such as *etagères* and bureaus are areas of pierced metal fretting and front legs cast in the form of writhing serpents. Some pieces, including a sewing machine, a piano with a musical box inside, and a child's desk, have cast metal details.

A creamy or white enamel finish was also used for parlor sets, kitchens, and bathroom suites. The bedroom sets are plain and a little gloomy, usually with low-ended beds, dark wardrobes, and "potty" cupboards. The salon suites are, however, extremely colorful with their bright silk upholstery buttoned in gold. There does not appear to have been any dramatic change of style towards the end of the 19th century. It is known that in comparison with other tin toy firms, the production methods of Rock & Graner were old-fashioned, and the quality remained excellent.

Baecker and Vaterlein has ascertained that the firm was not, as once thought, taken over by Märklin, but was dissolved entirely. Moreover, I have specific evidence that

RIGHT **Some Rock & Graner drawing room pieces, showing buttoned silk upholstery, and including a jardinière.**

the firm of Georg Kühnrich, of Waldheim in Saxony, bought machines and factory equipment from Rock & Graner in 1905, and was making dollhouse furniture, including a washstand identical to Rock & Graner's, as late as 1926.

Another firm, whose wares have not as far as I know been distinguished from those of Rock & Graner, was Henry Blumhardt of Stuttgart, Germany, which also exhibited at the 1851 Crystal Palace Exhibition, showing "a collection of toys made of japanned tin, lead, pewter, bronze, iron, and wood."

In the 1880s, an intrepid English journalist, Mrs. Brewer, published an account in *The Girls' Own Paper* of her visits to the toy-making centers of Germany, including the factories of Rock & Graner and Blumhardt, giving a description of the manufacturing process. She notes that at Rock & Graner, the painting was done by women and girls "for which work they are educated from earliest infancy." The better pieces were painted and stoved up to 15 times before completion.

At Blumhardt's she met the widowed proprietor, "who gives out the material herself, and her eye scans all the finished work . . . The toys which she and her son send into the world are all of metal richy upholstered – among which are dollhouses with furniture complete.

Some American Makers

Before the second quarter of the 19th century, America seems to have relied considerably on Europe for toys; small tin wares were made in Maine and other areas, but these were also imported from Wolverhampton. These kitchen toys, decorated with the varnish colors known as asphaltum and painted with floral patterns on black grounds, are very charming.

The first dollhouse wooden furniture seems to have been made in Hingham, Massachusetts, by William Sewell Tower, in direct competition with European exports. Born in 1826, he founded the Tower Toy Guild in 1860. This was an association of craftsmen, including Samuel and Caleb Hersey, who made tables, stools, cradles, washstands, and other wooden furniture. Two younger members of the Guild, Loring Hersey Cushing and Augustus L. Hudson, were still working in 1914.

BELOW **A selection of early American chairs. Of particular note are three cast iron chairs sold by Ellis Britton & Son and Stevens and Brown (top row, nos 1, 3, and 4) and a tinplate chair advertised by Althof, Bergmann and Co. (middle row, no 3). (*Courtesy of the Washington Dolls' House and Toy Museum.*)**

More sophisticated, and decidedly urban in style, are the early products of the American tinplate manufacturing companies, which were of course famous for their "boys' toys" and their clockwork output. Francis, Field & Francis was in operation in Philadelphia by the early 1840s, and soon afterwards there was a substantial industry in Connecticut, with New York as the commercial center. Stevens & Brown of Cromwell, Connecticut, and Ellis Britton & Eaton of Springfield, Vermont, both appear to have made tin toy furniture in the 1870s in high Victorian revived rococo style, upholstered in a flock imitation of velvet.

Flora Gill Jacobs has pointed out in her remarkable book *Dolls' Houses in America* that the obscure commercial relationships between these firms make attributions difficult and perplexing. Imitation wood graining was employed by these firms, which may well have been aware of Rock & Graner and Evans & Cartwright. Their catalogs illustrate dining room, parlor and bedroom suites, and Mrs. Jacobs also illustrates a delightful toy office set in yellow graining.

Althof, Bergman & Co., of New York, also manufactured tin parlor, dining room, kitchen, and bedroom furniture with stenciled decoration in the 1870s. Hull & Stafford of Clinton, Connecticut, was in operation during the same period. In addition, similar pieces were also made in cast iron, a material used virtually only in America, by the same firms that produced tin wares. All these early toys are extremely rare, even in America, by comparison with German toys of the same period.

Amateur Toy Makers

~

Some mention must be made of the toys made at home by amateurs, which found their way into many dollhouses. These were sometimes sold by ladies at fund-raising bazaars. Marbled or gilt paper was a favorite material, covering the cardboard used to construct tiny items such as needlecases in the shape of harps, pianos, or even an organ. The more skilled ladies attempted quilling, or coiled paper work. Pieces of furniture, including fancy chairs and sofas, could be made out of quills from geese or other fowl, which, partly or wholly stripped of the feathers, were fastened together with pins. Beads were worked in bright floral patterns to make miniature pincushions, or were combined with fabric to make upholstered chairs.

BELOW **Feather chairs, the large one with an amusing "Mackintosh" appearance. English, date uncertain.**

Queen Victoria and Baroness Lehzen made little fabric-covered cardboard chairs, stools, and dressing tables for the little wooden dolls they dressed at Kensington Palace, London.

All of these handmade novelties and more were introduced to the dollhouse in the late 18th and 19th centuries, and the collector should seek them, as they are even more evocative of the period than objects made commercially.

ABOVE **A pincushion, in the form of a Regency rosewood table.**

FROM THE MID-19TH CENTURY TO 1914

CHAPTER 3

ABOVE **Examples of Bliss
furniture, lithographed paper on
wood, decorated with child
figures.**

RIGHT **A tinplate shower, baby's bath, umbrella stand, and continental stove with transfer decoration, of types produced by many German manufacturers.**

BELOW **A tinplate fireplace with pierced detail, probably Märklin.**

It was in this era of great wealth and security for the middle classes that the commercial production of items for the dollhouse expanded in a bewildering variety. As the 19th century wore on, real houses were filled with an increasing clutter of furniture and bric-à-brac, and dollhouses reflected this trend.

More advanced industrial processes, combined with the exploitation of many of the workers in Germany, also meant vast quantities of goods could be produced at ever cheaper prices. The clever use of techniques such as color lithography improved the appearance, while disguising simplified construction. Nevertheless, for the collector this remains the golden age, when everything that appeared in the real home could be found in toyshops for a matter of pennies.

The dollhouse furniture collector is not, however, so well able as the collector of expensive toys such as toy trains or dolls to identify the origins of particular pieces. The more expensive toys were often made by large specialized firms

that produced their own catalogs, which can now be obtained in reproduction.

The cheap wooden and metal pieces were produced in Germany mainly by small firms based in little towns and villages. They might produce a range of different toys in a single material – for example, in the Erzgebirge area mainly wood was used. They relied on homeworkers to turn out the goods, and agents and wholesalers to market their wares abroad.

Catalogs were produced by the agents, but although these sometimes make it possible to ascribe a type of furniture to a particular country, it does not help to find the maker. A trademark on a piece is a rarity, and anonymity the norm. There has also been far less research into these toys than into German dolls, trains, or cars.

Märklin of Göppingen, Württemberg, Germany, is an example of a well-known firm which, because of its other products, has been well documented. Founded in 1859 to make metal equipment for doll's kitchens, and run by Mrs. Caroline Märklin for many years until her sons took over the business in 1888, it has been renowned for high-quality metal toys, especially railways, until the present day.

Its 1895 catalog shows a wide range of tinplate items for doll's kitchens, some of them in small enough sizes for a dollhouse. A much wider range, including kitchen and bathroom pieces, fireplaces, stoves, radiators, cribs, café tables, plant stands and hat stands is shown in the 1900 catalog. Typical is the use of bent metal rods and metal fretwork in ornate designs, which were gilded or enameled, with transfer decoration. These pieces are very strong and well made.

Metal Furniture

—— ~ ——

Gebrüder Bing of Nuremberg, Germany, the other giant metal toy company, was also very active in the toy kitchen field, supplying complete kitchens in metal, or wood and metal, and children's stoves. Very attractive sets of kitchen furniture, enameled and decorated with flowers, are shown in catalogs of the early 1900s, but all are in the larger scale suited to toy kitchens.

Many other small firms made tin furniture, enameled and sometimes with lithographed decoration, but their products are difficult to identify. One very sizeable firm, Kindler & Briel of Böblingen, Württemberg, Germany, founded in 1865, produced large toys such as elegant shops in wood and metal, and also made accessories including metal flower stands, beds, and gramophones. The firm is still in operation.

A number of other German firms produced cast pewter accessories, including chandeliers, lamps, clocks, and dinner services. In fact, the variety of these accessories is almost limitless, ranging from cigar cutters to wine jugs in metal mounts, from sewing machines to elegant ladies embracing mantel clocks. Among the known firms are F.W. Gerlach of Naumberg, founded in 1865 and operating until 1939, G. Sohlke of Berlin, which exhibited at the 1851 Crystal Palace Exhibition in London, and F.K. Martin.

There were also many other firms, some making domestic pieces as a sideline from the popular flat tin solders. Enormous quantities of these pressed pieces were made throughout this period up to 1939, and they are still obtainable. Rare pieces include firescreens with lithophanes (transparent porcelain pictures) inset, and the more elaborate light fittings. Mainly for the German market, these firms also

BABETTE SCHWEITZER

Another specialized metal firm, Babette Schweitzer of Diessen, Germany, established almost 200 years ago, is still in existence. It works in cast pewter, usually in filigree style. The old pieces are often very soft, but modern pieces from the same molds seem harder. Items such as chests of drawers, dressing tables, cribs, baby carriages, fireplaces and stoves, dating from the late 19th century in style, are very pretty, although sometimes difficult to fit in with other types of furniture. Accessories such as mirrors, picture frames, and birdcages are among the most successful objects, and appear in most houses.

ABOVE **Cast pewter chairs and settee, two with a fine detailed leaf pattern, for use in a conservatory. German.**

made miniature church fittings, in order to adorn the popular toy altars.

Brass accessories from the mid-19th century on tended to be gilded, to match the opulent interiors of the period. The brightness and enduring quality of the gilding is remarkable, and the pressings are crisp and well finished. Clocks, candlesticks, oil lamps, mirrors, and picture frames are not uncommon. Birdcages and firescreens make attractive accessories. Highly sought after are chandeliers and other light fittings. The origin of all these is unknown at present, although a boxed set with a lithographed lid with "E & S" on it appeared at a Christie's auction. Pewter pieces were also gilded, and so were some steel and tinplate. Märklin gilded some of its metal accessories.

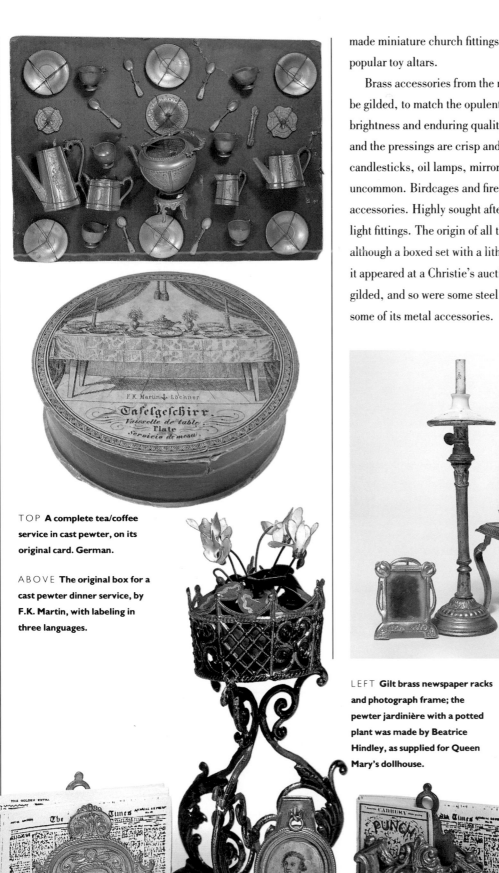

TOP **A complete tea/coffee service in cast pewter, on its original card. German.**

ABOVE **The original box for a cast pewter dinner service, by F.K. Martin, with labeling in three languages.**

LEFT **Gilt brass newspaper racks and photograph frame; the pewter jardinière with a potted plant was made by Beatrice Hindley, as supplied for Queen Mary's dollhouse.**

ABOVE **Gilt brass pieces, including a table, birdcage with glass bird, standard oil lamp, Art Nouveau mirror and fine quality early clock.**

RIGHT **Victorian needlecases, a cardboard and bone piano, 1830–40, and a W. Avery gilt brass worktable and footstool.**

BELOW **The mark of W. Avery & Son on the base of a footstool.**

A distinctive type of gilt brass furniture, in a late 19th-century style of imitation bamboo, with red silk upholstery, known as "Tiffany" in America, remains a mystery. It has been ascribed to Märklin, but does not appear in its catalogs; Nora Earnshaw has suggested a French firm, Banneville et Aulanier.

The English firm of W. Avery & Sons of Redditch had the great merit of clearly marking most of its wares, which are also gilt brass. A firm of needle manufacturers, it turned in the mid-19th century to making fancy patent needlecases, in the shape of small pieces of furniture, including chairs, cradles, and easels. The potential of these items for the

dollhouse must have been quickly recognized and mother's sewing box frequently raided. They are sought after by collectors of needlework accessories, and so have become expensive. In the 1840s, a foundry, in the town of Gleiwitz, in what is now part of Poland, produced some unusual Gothic-style chairs in bronze and cast iron, which were originally intended as pincushions.

Other continental suites of furniture, usually said to be Viennese, were made in heavy gilt metal, brass or bronze, inset with enamel panels decorated with scenes in an insipid, pseudo-18th century style. These are cabinet pieces that were not intended for a dollhouse, and are not really suitable for it.

LEFT **Gilt brass mock-bamboo furniture, with silk upholstery, c.1900.**

LEFT **A bronze Gothic chair, with its original pincushion seat and animal arms and feet. Gleiwitz, Poland, 1846.**

ABOVE **A needlecase decorated with charming puppies in velvet.**

RIGHT **Three turned and carved bone ("ivory") pieces, the smallest on a blonde wood cabinet with scrap decoration.**

Bone and Ivory Furniture
~

An elegant German specialty, also tending towards the decorative souvenir rather than a child's toy, was bone or ivory furniture, mainly the former. Often thought to be oriental, a German agent's catalog of about 1840 auctioned by Sotheby's showed a number of pieces partly stained in brown, including antlers, suitable for hunting box rooms. The firm of Wittich, Kemmel & Co. of Geislingen, Württemberg, Germany, exhibited pieces at the 1851 Crystal Palace Exhibition, London. Later this work also became a specialty of the Wennemayer family of Berchtesgaden, who continued production until the turn of the century. The furniture, which is displayed at Berchtesgaden, appears very small scale.

Larger, more elaborate pieces with pierced fretwork of a very standardized sort was produced in large quantities probably until a bit later, but the firm concerned is not known with any certainty. There are, however, pieces with the name of the small German resort of Grund in the Harz area included in the design, which are, presumably, souvenir ware. These pieces were popular with Queen Mary, the current Queen Elizabeth's grandmother, who furnished a miniature room with them. Their exquisite but unrealistic detail does not, however, combine well with most toy furniture.

LEFT **Penny toys, including a German tinplate globe, stroller, and a Meier sewing machine; a French pewter chair and pushchair.**

Penny Toys

~

A number of French and German firms specialized in the "penny toys," which were made to be sold very cheaply, sometimes by street vendors or in shops as Christmas decorations. In his recent book, David Pressland writes that the peak years for these toys were between 1890 and 1914. Both the cast alloy and the lithographed tin sorts provided items intended for the dollhouse. Lithographed tin baby carriages and high chairs were sold complete with tin occupants, but sewing machines, gramophones, birdcages, and coal scuttles were suited to doll's rooms, and tin globes are found in schoolroom settings.

Mainly German firms, such as Meier, Distler and Fischer, made the tin toys, but the cast lead alloy toys were made in France by Simon et Rivollet and other firms. These include a very wide range of furniture, 1 inch or so long, but with no uniform scale. Thus the clocks and candelabra will fit into a 1:12 house, but the chairs, settees, strollers, and beds will suit only the tiny lithographed houses of the same period.

RIGHT **Blond wood group with blue sateen upholstery, small scale. German c.1870–80.**

They are easy to find and are painted in a standard range of colors, often green. The bath chair for invalids is perhaps the most unusual.

While metal production showed a great increase in this period, most furniture, of course, continued to be made of wood. The principal areas of production were in Saxony and Thüringia, Germany, although towards the end of the century other countries made some input. The styles gradually changed, although conservatism ensured that one sort overlaps with another.

The mid-century saw the introduction of furniture in very light wood finishes, with curving lines and pale silk or cotton upholstery, or decorated with brightly printed scraps. The rosewood finishes continued, but the transfer decorations were now more ornate and the outlines more fanciful, with bulbous turnings on the legs.

CHROMO-LITHOGRAPHY

RIGHT **High-quality, lithographed paper on wood drawing room group, decorated with cherubs and children, dated 1880 on original box.**

ABOVE **Small-scale German lithographed paper on wood, c.1880, imitating inlaid ebonized furniture.**

RIGHT **An unusual suite, with lithographed paper decorations behind glass. German, 1880–90.**

The invention of chromo-lithography earlier in the century and its use later on to make decorative papers, were responsible for the development in the 1870s and 1880s of specially printed decorations covering whole suites of furniture. Some of these are a riot of flowers, birds, and even animals or cherubs, possibly imitating Berlin woolwork, but perhaps just fanciful.

Other suites are decorated in geometric designs, presumably intended to represent inlays. The styles are usually revived rococo, with bulbous turned legs. The makers are unknown, although an attractive suite has been found with the monogram CDL or DCL, possibly representing a Leipzig printing firm.

Changing Styles

The 1870s saw the beginning of a reform movement in real furniture, when, in Britain, Charles Eastlake castigated the over-stuffed, formless upholstery of the revived rococo style. In Germany this reform resulted in a return to Renaissance historical styles, just as elaborate but with stiffer outlines and the use of heavily carved oak. Dollhouse manufacturers followed the trend enthusiastically, and continental doll-houses rejoiced in rooms filled with large oak pieces of a very masculine appearance, well suited to Bavarian hunting lodges.

New styles followed rapidly towards the end of the century, with the use of pearwood (a yellowish color), walnut, cherry, red stain and, influenced by the vogue for Japanese style, an ebony black. Upholstery was often plush, velvet, or imitation leather. Handles were frequently made in pewter. It is a curious fact that while many of these styles would be cumbersome or oppressive in life size, in miniature their very elaboration and strong character brings back the past in a vivid and attractive way. Dollhouse furniture never copies the best designers, but is an exact guide to the most popular and trite styles.

Art Nouveau, that extravagant fashion of the 1890s, had only a minimal effect on the furniture, which continued to reflect Victorian modes up to World War I, although the use of green-stained wood and the occasional sinuous wave shows that manufacturers were aware of the trends.

Bamboo suites were common, but are often too large and crude to be attractive. The successful introduction of bent wood furniture by Thonet had an immediate effect, with sets of black-stained chairs and tables with wicker seats being widespread. A new interest in hygiene and light in the home led to the use of white and cream for bedroom, kitchen and bathroom furniture, often with gilt lines or restrained transfer decoration.

In addition to Gebrüder Schneegas of Waltershausen, Germany, whose catalogs for this period exist but have not been reprinted, and which made a popular yellow cherry range, a number of other large firms were set up in the 1890s in Saxony. No fewer than 14 firms making furniture were operating in Eppendorf in 1911. Paul Leonhardt of this town specialized in furniture in boxed sets, but also made rooms, shops and other wooden toys, which were continued by the firm after World War I. Details are given in the next chapter. Paul Hunger and Richard Auerbach were also based in Eppendorf, and continued after the war. Other firms are listed on pages 76 to 79, but in only a few cases has it so far been possible to attribute actual examples accurately.

RIGHT **Red-stained furniture, German 1900–20, with a velvet covered settee, c.1900.**

RIGHT **An Art Nouveau**
cabinet; left, a sofa and cabinet
showing the influence of the
Wiener Sezession style.

LEFT **Green-stained wood,**
German, *c.*1900; green glass
goblets of the same period.

RIGHT **A yellow cherry**
bedroom, attributed to
Schneegas, *c.*1900, showing
typical steam-pressed decoration
on wood.

Glassware and China

~

Glassware of every description was made in Lauscha, in Thüringia, Germany, from the early part of the century, the town specializing then as now in artisan glass-making, and in Bohemia. It is unlikely that Venice was involved in this production. The products included wine bottles, glasses, jugs, tea sets in milk glass with painted flowers, fittings for lamps, and vases. Glass birdcages with colored glass birds are particularly pretty.

ABOVE **A Limoges porcelain toilet set and two pen-and-ink trays. The lower jug and basin are identical to those supplied for Queen Mary's doll's house.**

ABOVE **An assortment of glass, including two spun glass items, a milk glass cup and saucer, a lemon squeezer, a syphon and bottle, and a drinking glass set in pewter, Lauscha and/or Bohemia.**

It is sometimes difficult to distinguish old glass from modern pieces, but the original appears more delicate and less regular. Other items which find a place in a dollhouse include the mat molded glass "Tiffany" cats and dogs, with crystal eyes and metal collars. Bears, monkeys and other animals were also made, although not, of course, by the famous American company. Glass flowerpots containing paper plants are of the same type. Some of the smaller items were originally intended as toys in Christmas crackers.

In Germany, turned wooden sets imitating china continued to be made, either decorated with tiny flowers, or with painted rings in blue and other colors. Real china services, often in a blue and white pattern derived from the Meissen "onion," were also available from Germany, while tea, coffee, chocolate, and toilet sets were produced in the Limoges factories in France. The latter are now expensive, as they are carefully modeled and painted porcelain miniatures. Another luxury accessory is the Viennese bronze plant in a

pot, cold-painted by hand, of which deceptive reproductions are now on the market. Originals are sometimes marked "Austria" or "J.H." or "R & G", and many probably date from the period between 1900 and 1930.

German products were exported world-wide in this period, and it was usual for labels, for example, on kitchen storage jars to be printed in four languages (English, French, Spanish, and German), leading to confusion in the past over the origin of such items. Other countries also produced items but mainly on a smaller scale for domestic consumption.

In Britain, a small amount of rather heavily built, unmarked mahogany furniture was made in the mid-19th-century, notably by a firm which supplied Mrs. Bryant for her large house of 1860, now in the Bethnal Green Museum, London. This large-scale furniture was upholstered in buttoned velvet and must have been expensive; it was made commercially and was not exclusive to Mrs. Bryant.

BELOW **Frosted glass dogs, with crystal bead eyes and metal collars with tags.**

RIGHT **Fretwork furniture with gilt and scrap paper trim, of the type usually seen in "French" open rooms.**

ABOVE **A collection of Viennese bronze flowers in pots.**

In France, dollhouses were not popular as toys, but doll's rooms were sold furnished in a uniform way, with fretcut-outline suites, white with gilt trimming and upholstered in pink or blue silk. However, this furniture was also sold with a type of lithographed dollhouse similar to known German houses, and the question of its origin is unresolved. Some commercially made fretwork furniture is also said to be French, but this, too, is unproven.

ABOVE **Mahogany Mrs Bryant drawing-room pieces. English, 1860s.**

LEFT **Adrian Cooke chairs and rocker; the label under the seat reading: "The 'Fairy' Furniture – Indestructible – An alloy of Aluminum & White Metal – Manufactured by Adrian Cooke Metallic Works Chicago, Ill. Patent applied for."**

Activity in America

~

Small amounts of dollhouse furniture seem to have been made in Sweden, Finland, Austria, Bohemia, which produced painted peasant styles, and in Russia, but this is seldom available outside the country of origin. In America, however, a major toy industry was developing and commercially made dollhouses and furniture were soon in competition with imports.

The R. Bliss Manufacturing Company was founded in the 1830s, but the lithographed paper-on-wood furniture for which the firm is best known seems to have first appeared in the 1880s. It is brightly colored but was mostly produced in too large a scale to fit into the small Bliss houses. The Alphabet set is much like a nursery teaching toy. Other sets show children at play, or fanciful upholstery, all in paper.

Other American manufacturers continued to specialize in metal furniture. Peter F. Pia of New York made pewter alloy furniture, including room settings, in the 1890s. Adrian Cooke of Chicago labeled his aluminum alloy furniture as made in "The Fairy Toy Works." Other furniture was made in the less fairy-like material of cast iron: the firms concerned would have regarded this as only a small sideline from their large-scale production of trains and other metal toys.

In such a brief account it is hardly possible to do justice to the wealth of different items on sale at the end of the 19th century, but the illustrations help to convey the imagination and skill which went into the design and manufacture of quite cheap toys.

Sufficient pieces are still available to allow the collector to choose a style and size suited to a particular dollhouse and within a collecting budget. Walterhausen and top-quality tinplate furniture is always likely to be expensive, but the better-made suites from the turn of the century are affordable and full of character.

LEFT **A set of unusual painted furniture, with gilt paper and chenille decoration. Russian, 1900 or earlier. (*Courtesy of Christie's, London.*)**

LEFT **A carboard room with original furniture in pewter, probably by Peter F. Pia.** (*Courtesy of the Washington Dolls' House and Toy Museum.*)

DO-IT-YOURSELF

ABOVE **Bead furniture, probably homemade, the table legs made of carved oriental nuts.**

ABOVE **A shell-decorated cardboard dressing-table, stool and cabinet with stuffed animals, including a hyena.**

In the Victorian home, do-it-yourself items continued to be made, although not with quite such elegant results as in the earlier period. Magazines encouraged the making of furniture from beads threaded on wire or pins stuck into corks and covered with thread. Half-tester beds were made from matchboxes with the lids upended, neatly covered with fabric.

The decoration of small objects such as dolls with shells had long been a pastime, but the manufacturers of seaside souvenirs now made these commercially, with a cardboard base. They included sofas, chairs, dressing tables, picture frames with marine views, beds, and more fanciful articles such as a dog kennel complete with the front half of a bisque bulldog emerging. These items can often be dated from registered design numbers. "Fancy" furniture is difficult to blend with the more ordinary pieces, and may need a room to be decorated around it.

Another popular home activity from the 1890s was fretwork, in which elaborate pierced designs were attempted. The British firm of Hobbies Ltd, Dereham, Norfolk, northeast of London, published a weekly journal from 1895, which includes fretwork patterns for the work. In that year, designs for Chippendale furniture were offered for a shilling and sixpence (1s 6d; about 14 cents). The fashion for this work continued until well after World War I.

THE WARS
AND BETWEEN

CHAPTER 4

World War I, four years of conflict and death, was followed in 1918 by reparations from Germany to the victorious side and devastating inflation, culminating in the world-wide slump of the early 1930s. This brought an end to German dominance in the toy industry, and resulted in profound changes in Britain and America. All this is reflected in the history of toy furniture depicted in this chapter.

Initially, the effect of the war was to dry up the supply of German toys. French toy shop catalogs, which until 1914 had been full of German exports, including fully furnished blue roof type dollhouses, instead showed simple wooden toys made in France. By 1918 these were described as *jouets des mutilées de la guerre*. In Britain, the government encouraged new firms to set up, giving promises, not in the event honored, of protection from foreign competition after the war.

Wooden Furniture
——— ~ ———

A surprising number of these new British firms decided to make wooden dollhouse furniture, probably because it did not require the skills needed in metalworking. For example, the Parkstone Toy factory of Dorset, southwest England, made a range of furniture, Edwardian in style, to complement its houses. In 1917, J. Joseph of south London advertised cheap wooden furniture covered with printed paper.

Two ladies, Miss Palethorpe and Miss Copeman, of Liverpool, northwest England, made "artistic and practicable" furniture under the name of Homeland Toys, together with pretty Tudor houses. Mrs. Alfred Sabine, who started teaching toymaking as her share of war work, set up the Herne Bay Toy Factory and School of Toy-Making in

Kent, in the south of England, producing miniature dressers and kitchen ranges with all accessories, among other novelties. Lord Roberts Memorial Workshops, founded in 1899 and employing disabled ex-servicemen, was one of the few non-professional firms to survive after the war, but it stopped making toy furniture in 1923. Its products are often marked.

After 1918, firms were set up by and for returning soldiers. One of the first and most successful was Elgin Ltd. of Enfield, London, established in 1919 by Eric Elgin and his sisters, to employ ex-servicemen and munitions workers. The furniture was well-made and expensive, but what probably ensured its success, both with parents and collectors such as Queen Mary and Sir Neville Wilkinson, was that the styles were British, and not continental. Just as in the real furniture of the day, Jacobean, Queen Anne, Chippendale, Adam, and Sheraton were the periods favored for their aura of stability and good living. The furniture has an impressed mark "Elgin/Enfield."

By 1921, Lines Bros. Ltd. (Triang), casting around for some furniture to suit its new range of houses, appears to have arranged to market Elgin furniture under the name "Period Doll Furniture, Scale Model," said to be 1:12, although usually slightly less. In 1922, Lines had to reduce the price of these boxed suites, and it produced a cheaper line "by sacrificing a little of the detail." This includes a kitchen set, and was not marked by the factory. By 1926, Elgin appears to have closed down. Its products are popular with collectors wishing to furnish inter-war houses, as they go well with the post-war Tudor style of porridge wallpaper and faded chintz.

Nº 19442. Jouet des Mutilès de la Guerre.
SALLE à MANGER 4 pièces, bois laqué, décoration art nouveau, garnie d'un menage faïence.

Nº 19443. Jouet des Mutilés de la Guerre.
CHAMBRE à COUCHER 4 pièces, bois laqué, décoration art nouveau, garniture toilette en faïence de couleurs.

LEFT **From a French catalog of 1918, showing painted wooden furniture made by disabled soldiers, provincial in style, with Art Nouveau influence.**

LEFT **Some Triang Period pieces, late 1930s; the doll is listening anxiously to the news. (The table is not Triang.)**

Later on in the 1930s, a new range of furniture, under the same name, Period, but quite different, was brought out by Triang. It was made from extremely thin hardwood, in Queen Anne and Jacobean styles, including upholstery in small chintz patterns and a variety of accessories such as clocks and firescreens. It is more elegant but less durable than the sturdier Elgin, being rather brittle. It was even made in a kit form, a daunting project.

The furniture known as Westacre Village has something in common with Lines' 1930s Period, but is more amateur in construction, although better in style. Mrs. Burkbeck of Norfolk, Britain, set up a cottage industry in her village in about 1925 and subsequently sold the furniture, which was very expensive for the time, at Charles Morrell's shop in the Burlington Arcade, London.

The styles are generally 18th century in derivation, and many items, including chairs, tables and cupboards, were decorated in gilt in imitation of Chinese lacquer, on black, red, or green grounds. Brown finishes were also used. Upholstered suites in a 1920s style and standard lamps with hand-painted parchment shades are also typical of the period country house. At £3.60 ($6.50), the four-poster bed was well out of reach of the ordinary family. Most of the pieces would look in keeping in a country home in the 1990s.

Some similar developments, resulting in expensive but fine-quality toy furniture, were taking place in America. Tynietoy was started in 1920 by Marion Perkins and Amy Vernon, who, equipped initially with a child's circular saw, sold the furniture from their home in Providence, Rhode Island.

RIGHT **Westacre Village furniture, with lacquered items, and a hand-painted standard lamp shade.**

simple furniture in 1916, and the firm of Strombecker made solid walnut pieces in a small scale in the 1920s. Albert Schoenhut, the wonderful firm making dolls and circuses, also made hardwood furniture from 1928, initially in a walnut finish. Later finishes included flocked upholstery and a variety of painted finishes, such as green or orange kitchens, pink or green bedrooms, and white or mauve bathrooms. All

The styles chosen for the main rooms were 18th century, including Chippendale and Sheraton, and also American Colonial and early 19th century. There were also modern sets for the kitchen, a breakfast nook, handwoven rugs, and many other accessories. By 1930, they were employing 50 workmen and turning out excellent quality wooden pieces at very reasonable prices. Amazingly, this enterprise, according to Mrs. Jacobs, lasted until 1950.

All these wooden makes had pretensions to adult perfection, but ordinary children were not forgotten. In America, the Child's Welfare Co. of Chicago produced

ABOVE LEFT **Two rooms of the Tynietoy mansion, furnished mainly with Tynietoy pieces. (Courtesy of the Washington Doll's House and Toy Museum.)**

ABOVE **Strombecker walnut chairs. American, 1920s.**

ABOVE **The mark on a Strombecker chair.**

RIGHT **A set of lounge furniture by Schoenhut. (Courtesy of the Washington Dolls' House and Toy Museum.)**

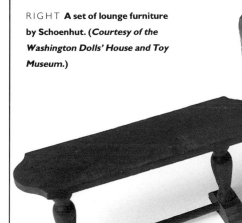

RIGHT **A green kitchen set by Pit-a-Pat; the stove is wooden.**

the pieces were chunky and suited the company's solidly made houses and bungalows. After various changes, including a smaller cheaper range, production finished in 1934.

Other, even cheaper furniture was made in pressed cardboard; a set made for the Dunham Company, a coconut firm, as an advertising device, is in the Margaret Woodbury Strong Museum at Rochester, New York. The collection of paper furniture is a fascinating topic which cannot be covered fully here, but many examples can be found in Europe and America, and some literature is listed in the Bibliography.

In Britain the same market was reached by several firms, the most important brand being the oddly-named Pit-a-Pat. E. Lehman & Co. was an import wholesaler in London, which in 1932 decided to manufacture 1:16 wooden furniture. At the British Industries Fair in 1933, Queen Mary, an avid collector as always, made some purchases, and the firm's success was assured. Production seems to have ceased during World War II, although the firm continued with other toy production at its factory postwar. Since large quantities were sold, the furniture is relatively easy to find. A good number of

BELOW **Pit-a-Pat and Tiny Toy living room pieces; note the "inlay" on the cutlery canteen.**

pieces are marked with oval or rectangular paper labels printed in red and black.

The styles are typical of 1930s suburbia, with chunky suites covered in dark brown rexine or velvet. Other furniture in dark brown stained wood has Tudoresque moldings, while the tea trolley and the canteen of cutlery have an 18th-century style inlay. Kitchen furniture was plain and also stained or painted green; bathrooms were white painted wood. There is little hint of the modern movement, apart from a tiled fireplace with a stepped outline.

Accessories provide the most interest in the range. The stained wooden radiogram is complete with record, movable pick-up and radio controls, and "Pit-a-Pat Radiogram" on the lid. There are also little packs of books called "the Pit-a-Pat Library," a brass gong with a black painted stand, and a dark wood fire screen with a floral transfer. Research by Gillian Kernon, Marion Osborne, and others has produced comprehensive information on these products.

Britain also had its Tiny Toy furniture, made in 1932–33, in two sizes, 1:16 and the 1:24 Duckie size (at this period England and America vied with each other for terrible names for their products). The suite was upholstered in real leather, and the furniture stained brown or painted red. Some unusual accessories, including a typewriter and an invalid table (a strange concept), were supplied in metal. The telephone was named "The Little Nuisance," and the toilet "The Usual Office."

Fretwork furniture continued to be popular, especially as a source of income for jobless ex-servicemen, and the firm of Handicrafts Ltd. of Kentish Town, London, published a number of dollhouse furniture designs, the earliest being for a bedroom in May 1914. Once a design had been published, it

ABOVE **A Tiny Toy telephone with a box, and a cast metal Charben's radio, both 1930s.**

continued to be available for many years, so dating is difficult. The firm also supplied kits of wood to be made up. The styles are mainly Art Nouveau, which has more scope for the fretworker than simpler designs.

In Germany, the wooden toy industry in Saxony and Thüringia recovered slowly, marketing its wares, as always, through agents at the great fairs at Leipzig and abroad. It struggled against new foreign toy industries and tariffs. While the small home workshops did not wholly disappear in the Erzgebirge area, much of the furniture output now came from a few large factories in Eppendorf, some of which were mentioned in Chapter 3.

RIGHT **Handicrafts fretwork furniture, made from a kit, 1920s.**

PAUL LEONHARDT

ABOVE **A cake shop, with furniture by Paul Leonhardt, c.1925, as advertised in the** **Universal Toy Catalog. (*Courtesy of Christie's, London.*)**

Paul Leonhardt, whose portrait is shown here, started his business in a small way in 1894, taking a share of a shoe factory to make toys and kitchen equipment initially. After 1900, dollhouse furniture became a specialty, together with cases for clocks and gramophones. In 1909 the Eppendorf factory burnt to the ground in mysterious circumstances, but was rebuilt in the most modern way.

When World War I broke out, the factory was partly requisitioned for military production. After the war the two sons of the owner, Erich and Herbert, joined the staff, and Paul became the overseas representative. His firm employed 100 workers in the factory and even more outworkers, and specialized in boxed sets of furniture, as well as making rooms, shops, and children's furniture.

Thanks to several color pages of advertisements in the reprinted 1924–26 Universal Toy Catalog of John Hess (Firm code no. 50), Leonhardt's range for these years can be clearly identified. One of the most attractive furniture

sets, 565/14, can be seen in the illustration above. German styles in furniture had changed less than those of other countries at this date. The overall impression as regards sitting rooms and dining suites is of very heavy pieces with carved or applied decoration, which some people find difficult to accept as products of the 1920s. A particularly characteristic piece is the upholstered show-wood sofa, which fits into a very large overmantel with cupboards at the side, a wholly continental concept.

Furniture was offered in light and dark oak, maple, beech and white varnish, and upholstered in satin, silk, or velvet. The more expensive sets had applied gilt metal decorations, including gilt wreaths. An elegant variant on the white suite illustrated was supplied in gilt wood with white satin upholstery. Scales varied from tiny cheap sets to what appears to be 1:6. Also manufactured were shops, rooms, kitchens, and market stalls.

Paul Hunger and his sons, Max and Gotthard, also manufactured on a large scale in Eppendorf, Germany, where they employed 120 workers. They made children's furniture and musical toys and games as well as dollhouse boxed sets, which were their specialty. They advertised the most modern styles, but were not represented by John Hess, so no color catalog is available. However, judging by black and white photographs, their style seems plainer than Leonhardt's. For instance, they made some very attractive toy summerhouses decorated with flowers in pots.

The products of Richard Auerbach and Richter & Wittich, also of Eppendorf, are known only from black and white illustrations, too. Both companies produced boxed sets in the same rather rectangular style, with tall sofas and tall sideboards, and fairly sparse decoration. Other Saxon firms are listed on pages 78–79, of which only Carl Brandt of Gössnitz features in The Universal Toy Catalog (firm's reference No. 39, pages 145 and 297), with, for example, "a dining room, imitated sculpture, corroded havana color, spreaded over with green velvet in an antique style".

RIGHT **A leatherette sofa fitted into an elaborate surround with cupboards; probably Leonhardt, c.1920. A German pewter stein and wine jug.**

RIGHT **A leatherette sofa fitted into an elaborate surround with cupboards; probably Leonhardt, c.1920. A German pewter stein and wine jug.**

Moritz Gottschalk of Marienberg, Germany, the old-established maker of dollhouses, mostly red roof at this period, also made furniture, using an inexpensive pressed cardboard painted in various colors, including white, red and brown. This furniture, illustrated in The Universal Toy Catalog (firm's reference No. 7, page 141), can be recognized by its slightly flexible quality, and was made in two scales. Outside Saxony, some new firms had started up, including Ulmer Holz und Spielwaren Werkstatten, of Ulm an der Donau, Württemberg. This firm made elegant furniture with simple lines and a more modern feeling, to furnish its Villa Puppenheim. It even produced a living room in the revived Biedermeier style, which was the latest German fashion (Universal Toy Catalog firm's reference No. 119, pages 310–311).

German furniture of this period is often mistaken for *fin-de-siècle* or Edwardian, and looks well in the later Christian Hacker houses or even those of G. & J. Lines, as well as Moritz Gottschalk red roofs. The best of it is finely made and extremely collectible.

Another country had in the meantime begun to challenge the western nations in the toy trade: imports were flooding in from Japan. Since the furniture of East and West has little in common and the Japanese had traditionally made fine lacquered pieces solely for the celebration of the Festival of Dolls, dollhouse furniture was not a major export. There was, however, an interesting line of wooden pieces inlaid with views of Mount Fuji and other scenes, in natural or stained veneers.

According to Gillian Kernon's research, the export of this furniture had begun before World War I and continued, with some deterioration, until 1939. The styles are a mixture of Japanese and European, and the decoration, which is sometimes wholly geometric, was purely Japanese. It remains an inexpensive collector's purchase.

ABOVE **Red-painted cardboard furniture, 1:16 scale, by Moritz Gottschalk of Marienberg, Germany.**

ABOVE **A Japanese telephone (possibly for cigarettes), hall stand, piano and chair, with other items shown on box lid marked "K K."**

Metal Furniture

~

Another aspect of the inter-war period is the production of furniture in metal, usually die-cast and often small in scale. The die-cast techniques had, of course, been used for toys for many years, notably by William Britain for toy armies, but the use of similar methods for furniture, as distinct from small metal accessories of the kind made by Gerlach, became common only after World War I. In many ways this is a far less suitable and decorative than the lithographed tin plate also commonly in use for toys since the 1890s, but the potential of the latter was for some unknown reason not fully utilized, and printed tin furniture is scarce.

William Britains is a firm that was founded in 1845 in Hornsey, London, and produced hollow-cast soldiers from the 1890s. As early as 1906, the firm was advertising an output of 5 tons of toys per week, and showed a cast-metal miniature baby chair that converts to a rocker, apparently a copy of the similar French penny toy. A bath chair, pots and pans, kettles, dishcovers, coal scuttles, and a few other items were added to the selection.

This dollhouse range seems to have continued unchanged for many years, being shown in 1939, and even made into the 1950s. It is remarkable that such an enterprising firm was content to make these few, rather overscale kitchen things. From 1909, the Reka Co. Ltd., of London made somewhat similar pieces, which are well marked "C.W. Baker, Reka Ltd., Made in England" on the base and which continued in production until at least 1933.

Charbens, founded in 1926 and noted for soldiers and circus figures, introduced fairly well-modeled cast furniture, on a 1:24 scale. Somewhat similar, but not as well produced sets were introduced in 1934 by Kew's Ltd., another toy soldier firm, and called Modlets. These came in dining, kitchen and bedroom sets, the styles being old fashioned and the colors including a red-brown wood finish.

A little later, in 1936, Meccano Ltd. introduced a dollhouse called Dolly Varden with miniature 1:24 die-cast furniture in four suites as part of its die-cast Dinky Toys range. Because of the prestige of the Meccano/Hornby firm, this has become the best-known metal furniture, although there is little justification for this.

ABOVE **Tootsietoy kitchen set, cast metal. American, 1920–30.**

The house was of flimsy, folding cardboard, and the furniture, unknown to the company, contained the seeds of its own destruction, in that the alloy used was unstable and could disintegrate in time. Where it has survived intact, it is very neatly cast and attractively painted in a choice of two color schemes for each suite, but much too small to be a satisfactory toy. The bathroom, with its linen basket with opening lid, and its basin with polished metal mirror, is the best set. Production ceased in 1940.

The American equivalent, unfortunately called Tootsietoy, after the daughter of the owner, Tootsie Dowst, is somewhat of an improvement on Dinky. Introduced by Dowst Manufacturing Co. of Chicago in the early 1920s, it continued for many years and in many variants. In 1923 the parlor set was gilt, the bedroom set blue, and the dining room set brown oak finish. The size was a little bigger than Dinky and the outlines much more elegant, while the price per set was only 83 cents. In 1930 the living room furniture was flocked "like latest overstuffed furniture," and the dining room had a Chinese Chippendale look. Cardboard houses were made for it, which appear to have been more substantial than Dolly Vardens.

Taylor & Barrett is a less well-known name, but its products are more useful in the typical 1930s house than the small-scale, die-cast pieces. Founded in 1923 in Islington, London, the firm survived until it was closed down by the war in 1941. Products were confined to accessories and items that could realistically be made in metal, such as gas stoves, refrigerators and vacuum cleaners, to a scale of about 1:16. Some pieces are marked "T & B" in the mold. A complete list is available in *Barton's Model Homes* by Marion Osborne (see Bibliography).

ABOVE **A cast alloy, pink bathroom Dinky, for a Dolly Varden house, with original rubber mat. British, 1930s.**

BELOW **A small-scale Modlets cast-metal dining room suite with a radiogram.**

BELOW **A Taylor & Barrett ("T & B") fireplace, and a Barrett & Sons ("B & S") post-World War II stove and pans.**

TIN ROOMS

As previously noted, only a few firms used printed tinplate, perhaps because it is more suited to "fantasy furniture" than the plain inter-war style. The German firm of Reil, Blechschmidt & Müller of Brandenburg produced a series of small-scale tin rooms, each furnished with printed tin furniture. Rooms $5 \times 2\frac{1}{2} \times 3$ inches were also sold by Louis Marx in America in 1920 as a set of six, which could be stacked inside a cardboard house. The relationship between these two products is not clear, but they are not identical.

TOP **Six miniature tin rooms, the original furniture fitting into** slots. **Reil, Blechschmidt & Müller, Germany, 1920s.**

ABOVE **Newly Weds tin room with tinplate furniture by Louis Marx, with original box.** (*Courtesy of the Washington Dolls' House and Toy Museum.*)

LEFT **Box showing Gwenda trademark.**

BELOW **Holdfast enameled heavy tinplate set.**

ABOVE **Cardboard bathroom with original cast-iron furniture by Arcade. (Courtesy of the** *Washington Doll's House and Toy Museum.)*

Other German firms continued to make the larger scale tin furniture for toy kitchens, including Martin Fuchs, Clemens Kreher, and C.F. Dieterich. Kindler & Briel (Universal Toy Catalog, firm's reference No. 17, pages 116–17) produced a wide range of wood and metal toys, but was also more concerned with the larger scale toy shops and kitchens. Georg Kuhnrich reproduced at least some Rock & Graner items. A British company, A.S. Cartwright of Birmingham, made tinplate sets under the name Holdfast in the 1930s, including one set in a tubular steel Art Deco pattern, and later, under the tradename Gwenda, a small tinplate range copying the cast-metal Dinky sets, with which it can at a glance be confused.

Finally, cast iron was still used in America. Kilgore Manufacturing Co. of Ohio made a range of small items to retail at between 10 and 50 cents, and a Sally Ann nursery set in a box. The Arcade Manufacturing Co. of Illinois had a cheerful advertising campaign in the late 1920s, suggesting that its kitchen, bathroom, and bedroom sets were made by "The Tiny Arcadians," a pixie-like tribe. Its kitchen items, very heavy and well cast, copied actual branded commercial refrigerators and stoves of the period, and they are of interest to the collector for this reason. Not many of us have the space or inclination to collect old stoves or sinks, but in miniature they make a fascinating study.

Plastic Furniture

Plastics had been around since the end of the 19th century, and bakelite was widely used for practical wares at this time. In 1937 British Xylonite Co. Ltd. had the brilliant idea that the material could be used to make toy furniture in the dramatic curving shapes of Art Deco, and it produced Toy Town Furniture (no doubt the name was based on the popular children's radio series by S.G. Hulme-Beaman), under its tradename Bex. Sets were made in red, green, blue, and brown. This is for me the most imaginative product of the whole inter-war period; for once, the design is advanced and the material perfectly suited to it.

ABOVE **Elegant bakelite bedroom suite with steel mirror by Bex.**

1945 TO THE PRESENT

CHAPTER 5

ABOVE **An Amanda Ann living
room, with Louis Marx figures.**

The end of World War II was not the end of privations and austerity, especially in Europe, but it was a time in which people looked forward, rejecting the prewar past. New homes were furnished in a style reflecting modern art, and the clean lines of Scandinavia were much admired. New materials were rapidly accepted, especially as there were continuing shortages of wood.

The dollhouse world, as always, lagged behind the times, but there was at least considerable acceptance of plastics, as soon as these became available to the toymakers. Wood and plastic have continued in use side by side, but metal gradually became less common.

For the collector, this is the world of our own and our mothers' childhood toys, and a world in which toys came increasingly to be regarded as ephemeral items, to be thrown away in a month or two. But beware: in just a few years the things we may either discard or donate to charity will develop their distinct period charm. We will have forgotten that once people had white kitchens with red handles, or limed oak cabinets rather than fitted units, but the toys will remind us. They are thus treated here with the same respect as the expensive antiques discussed in the previous chapters.

It was also a period in which the toy industry has become increasingly internationalized, so that companies have their products designed in one country, made in another,

frequently in the Far East, and marketed world-wide. Furniture does not therefore reflect the taste of only one country, but often has been designed to appeal to as many people as possible, thus losing a lot of interest and individuality. In the 1970s and 1980s, much toy furniture was also aimed at the very young child, the characteristics being simplicity and bright colors. Fortunately, some firms continued to make more detailed and individual toys that are of interest to the collector.

Meanwhile, as described in Chapter 1, the adult interest in miniature houses had begun its dramatic development in America and England, leading to the production of new scale model furniture specifically for this market. This chapter will deal first with toy furniture since World War II, in the three categories of wood, metal and plastic, and then with some aspects of modern miniatures.

Wooden Furniture

~

In her comprehensive book, *Barton's Model Houses*, Marion Osborne describes how, on the day peace was declared in Europe, May 8, 1945, Albert Barton, who had a background in the toy trade, set up a factory in Wandsworth, London with four of his colleagues in the fire brigade. While still firemen, they had been making some toys under the name Peko, but

RIGHT **A Barton kitchen, with wash boiler by Barrett.**

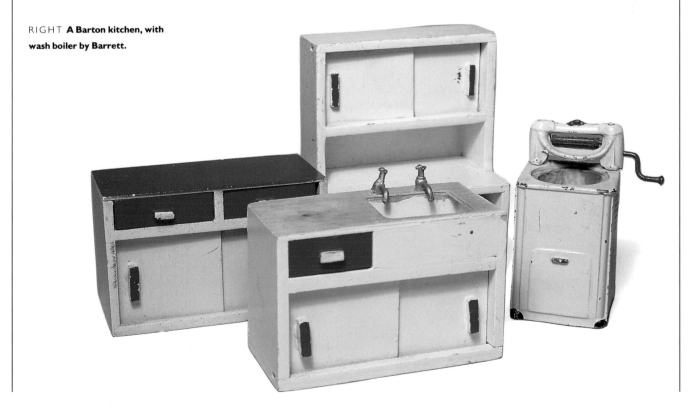

LEFT **Barton's Tudor range, four-poster (cover not original), court cupboard, monk's bench, chairs and wardrobe; dolls by Grecon, sold by Barton; gas fire by Taylor.**

the firm, A. Barton & Co. (Toys) Ltd., adopted a diamond-shaped mark incorporating "A.B. & Co."

The furniture was 1:16, made mainly of plywood with solid wood parts. The basic early ranges were in a medium wood stain, with plywood or card backs, and in the boxy, utility postwar styles. Nursery furniture was painted in pale blue or pink, and kitchens were green or off-white with distinctive wooden strip handles. A typical scheme is off-white with red handles. Slightly later models have pin-type handles, and turned brass handles were used from 1957. While well made and convincing, there is little to excite in these very masculine styles.

As early as 1948 Barton introduced its Tudor range, which was immediately popular and lasted, with one or two gaps, until 1984. Harking back to the 1920s Elgin style for inspiration, Barton recognized that suburban Britain had never stopped buying the Tudoresque type furniture, whatever forward-looking British designers thought of it. Pieces included, at various times, a Welsh dresser, a monk's bench, a chest, a court cupboard and a four-poster bed, all in a dark, polished-oak finish. It is decorated with beading and

impressed designs, including a typical diamond-shaped decoration. This furniture is often purported to be much older than it is, and in fact it does fit admirably into the smaller inter-war Tudor-style Triang or Amersham houses.

From very early in the firm's development, Barton sold a wide range of accessories, which enliven the rather worthy furniture. The company made some items itself, such as the cutlery box with metal or plastic cutlery, but others were made by small firms or individual workers. Some of these are mentioned under metal furniture on page 62; others include long-term favorites such as goldfish in a tank and a birdcage on a stand. The whole range was updated and pruned regularly, with the wood finishes becoming lighter, and plastic doors appearing in the kitchen in 1970.

RIGHT **Barton's Caroline's Home furniture; a Grecon gentleman plays the electronic organ.**

RIGHT **A Dol-Toi boxed kitchen and living room, including a wash boiler and television.**

BELOW RIGHT **A Dol-Toi set of cast-metal pans with food. British, 1960s.**

In 1975 the firm, which was in a more competitive market, introduced a new tradename and image with Caroline's Home, which was an attractive, open-access house with electrical fittings. The kitchen was completely redesigned in yellow with plastic chairs on a swivel base; the bathroom was lurid pink plastic, but the solid wooden construction remained for the living room and bedrooms. One piece of the Tudor range still continued: the sideboard in the boxed Windsor Lounge. Barton carried on until 1984, when it sold out to Lundby, which continued with the Caroline's Home range until recently. The early 1980s probably represented the nadir of children's interest in dollhouses.

For the collector, Barton represents middle of the road British taste over 40 years, with very well made and typical pieces. A personal favorite is a late piece, the electronic organ on which "Caroline's" grandfather regularly makes the lounge unbearable.

Dol-Toi Products (Stamford) Ltd. started in 1944 in one of Britain's most beautiful towns. Like Barton, it grew and obtained a major export trade. It was taken over by a consortium in 1974 and ceased trading in 1978. Made in 1:16 scale of beech wood, the furniture nevertheless seems smaller and is less detailed than Barton's, with which it can be confused. It is usually marked with a round label "Dol-Toi, Stamford" or "Dol-Toi Made in England."

Here, too, the accessories are more interesting than the furniture, and the metal tea set in pink or blue, the kitchen sets of pans with food, the leopard-skin rug, and that famous icon of postwar homes, the set of three plaster ducks in flight, are very collectible. There are also bookcases with sets of books, all with nursery rhyme titles.

LEFT **Rellaw Art Deco style pieces, probably 1940s.**

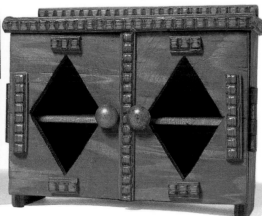

After the war the German Democratic Republic, in which the traditional toymaking areas were located, continued to export dollhouse furniture, but not on the same scale as previously. The factories were taken over by large organizations, such as Vero in Olbernhau, Saxony, whose most familiar products were wooden sets in nostalgic peasant styles, similar to tourist souvenirs. Some well-made furniture was produced in the 1970s, marked "Saxony," in a dark brown stain, but it has not been possible to trace the origin. This has been sold as antique, but it has a hard, modern furniture finish.

In West Germany the most respected name is that of Bodo Hennig of Wildpoldsried, which produces finely detailed furniture, scaled about 1:12. Its outstanding Ambiente range is modern and postmodern in style, the kitchens being extremely professional in design.

Scandinavia was the world center for advanced furniture design in the 1950s and 1960s, and "Swedish modern" was the choice of most young couples. This area also produced some of the most successful toy furniture postwar and, because of the national traditions of using wood, combined this material with plastics in the most skillful way.

In Denmark, the best known firm is Hanse, which produced a series of furniture called Princess Veronique.

This combines a casual style and warm, bright colors with a few pieces in folk-art tradition. But the most successful company world-wide has been the Swedish firm of Lundby of Lerum, Sweden, which also had a factory in Blackpool, England, for some years. Far more than any other company, it provided a complete 1:16 environment, with sophisticated bathrooms, showers and saunas, kitchen and laundry equipment, playroom, swimming pool, and an especially varied and effective range of lighting.

Styles varied at any one time, but it is possible to see a progression from a fairly formal look in the 1970s to a more relaxed, upholstered, prosperous feeling in the 1980s. The child was encouraged to act out a fantasy of luxury: "Have a good look at the new elegant bed with the brass bedstead. Imagine snuggling into one yourself. Sweet dreams." Design, finish, and accurate scaling gave the fantasy substance.

Lundby is, in a sense, competing for the child's interest with the doll-sized world provided for Barbie and Ken, but the Lundby furniture is much more lifelike and interesting, even if the dolls are a trifle dull. Lundby is the furniture that reflects most accurately the furnishing tastes of northern Europe over the last 20 years.

BELOW **Lundby wooden dining suite and piano, plastic accessories.**

LEFT **A Vero boxed living room in old German farmhouse style.**

FURNITURE FROM THE FAR EAST

ABOVE **Chinese People's Republic traditional lacquered pieces from Shanghai.**

RIGHT **Royden furniture from Sri Lanka: daybed, screen and chest on stand, in traditional styles.**

The Far East has been mainly noted for plastics, but two wooden products are worth mentioning for their adherence to the traditions of their respective countries. From Sri Lanka in the early 1980s came Royden Furniture in natural hardwood, copying the furniture made in the area for plantation life, including screens and caned seats, well made at 1:12. From the Chinese People's Republic came a series of charming sets in imitation black lacquer with gold decoration, copying the furniture exported from China in the 19th century. These sets have also been the subject of "antiquing" by unscrupulous persons selling them as old.

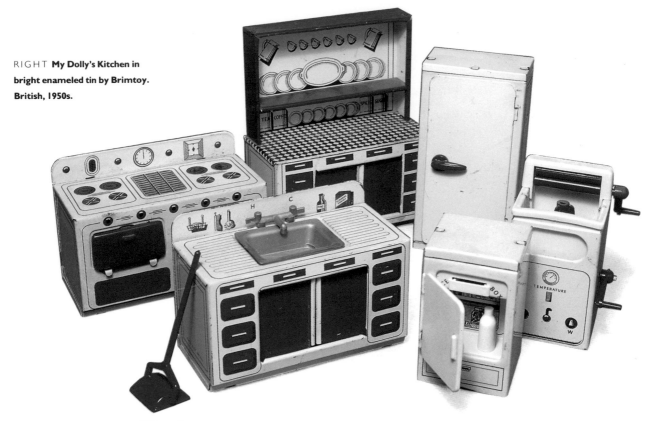

RIGHT **My Dolly's Kitchen in bright enameled tin by Brimtoy. British, 1950s.**

Metal

~

Tinplate in this period was regrettably on its way out as a material for toys, but a few firms continued to use it. Wells-Brimtoy Distributors Ltd., London, was the successor of a prewar firm founded in 1914, of which a complete account is included in *British Tin Toys* by Marguerite Fawdry. Mainly producing vehicles and trains, it is known by the dollhouse

BELOW **Lithographed tinplate rocking chair, probably Rico, Spain.**

enthusiast solely for its production of My Dolly's Kitchen in 1955. This included a dresser, stove, refrigerator, sink unit, washing machine and broom cupboard, all in printed tin, red on white. The kitchen table and chairs are plastic. The tiny scale just fits into the tin houses by Mettoy of the same period.

Less well known is the printed tin furniture by INGAP of Italy, a large firm founded in 1919. The date of these pieces is uncertain, but their appearance suggests that they are probably postwar. Like the French, the Italians have not had a tradition of dollhouses, which explains the shortage of examples from those countries.

An extrovert look was adopted by Kay (Sports and Games) Ltd., of London, a manufacturing company founded about 1935; its furniture is a combination of tinplate and hard plastic. The style, which could be described as high camp, uses, as one color scheme, yellow tinplate with black and lemon plastic, bent and twisted spirally.

Cast metal continued to be used for accessories. The prewar firm Taylor & Barrett split in two after the war, to form F.G. Taylor & Sons and A. Barrett & Sons (Toys) Ltd. Both firms supplied goods to Barton, and some were made from prewar molds. F.G. Taylor made gas and electric fires and a gas stove; the molded mark is "F.G.T." Barrett & Sons made dollhouse items from 1953, and eventually supplied Barton exclusively; it was wound up in 1983. Barrett also made a gas

LEFT **Barrett & Sons three ducks wall decoration. A little joke, "The Barretts of Sonderburg Road" (instead of** Wimpole Street!), is printed on the box. Barrett also supplied other firms.

stove, and other domestic appliances; its molded mark is "B. & S." Both firms later produced a variety of plastic items.

Shortly after the war, cast metal was used by two firms to produce small-scale sets of furniture. Fairylite was the tradename of Graham Bros., a London firm of importers founded in the 19th century, which marketed, inter alia, a cast-metal bathrooom set, usually in green. This is notable for having a working flush on its high-level toilet tank. Jacqueline was the tradename under which B. & S. (Mfg. & Distributing) Co. Ltd. sold sets of dining room and bedroom furniture, in red, green, blue and cream, made in Britain. It is not known which firm made them, but there is a cast logo on some pieces that appears to form the initials "G. I." The remarkable thing about these sets is that they are in full Art Deco style and are far more of the early 1920s than postwar. It is amusing to note that the ever-watchful Queen Mary snapped up a set of these at the British Industries Fair in 1948.

Two other London-based cast-metal manufacturers, Crescent and Johilco, also produced small quantities of cast-metal accessories, but the only other firm that has recently attempted a cast-metal range fairly soon abandoned the attempt. This was Mattel Inc. of Hawthorne, California, with The Littles, individual pieces of small-scale, very heavy metal with some plastic. The styles were 19th century, rather clumsy, and decorated with large floral transfers. Some small dolls and a house were available.

ABOVE **Fancy plastic and tin-plate by Kay. British, 1940s. German composition dolls, 1930s.**

LEFT **A lounge group of spray-painted steel, Art Deco style but made in the 1940s, by an unknown British company and sold under the name Jacqueline.**

RIGHT **Kleeware hard plastic, in 16:12 scale. British, 1950s.**

Plastic

~

Modern plastics were the chosen material of most manufacturers, as soon after the war as they could be obtained. Those available at first were hard and relatively brittle, but they were followed by cheaper, flexible kinds which were particularly used in the Far East.

A typical example is the British firm of O. & M. Kleemann Ltd., which, having been in the plastics business for many years, started to manufacture dollhouse pieces under the name of Kleeware in 1947. It is small-scale and was sold later with the Mettoy tin houses. The early pieces are hard plastic, typically in a dark brown or mid-blue color, and very well molded. Nursery items include a crib and a good see-saw. In the 1950s the firm changed over to flexible plastic in modern styles. Marion Osborne has established that the molds for this furniture were leased or sold to Renwal Toy Co. of America.

They also appear to have been used in Australia and Hong Kong, and sold under various names.

The furniture itself appeared in 1946, Renwal being one of the first firms in the US to use the material, and was available in cheap outlets until the 1960s. Well over 100 different items were produced in a variety of colors, including a wood finish. Another firm operating in the same period in Brooklyn, New York, was Plasco, which made hard plastic sets under the name Little Homemaker. The Reliable Toy Co. of Toronto, Canada, a doll manufacturer, also made good quality hard plastic pieces in about 1:12 scale.

The Ideal Novelty & Toy Co. of New York started in the 1940s with hard plastic in marbled brown and other colors, with Georgian-style living rooms and modern kitchens. They were marked "Ideal" or "Mfd. by Ideal Novelty and Toy Co. Made in U.S.A." In 1964 this company decided that the time was right for a more expensive, detailed type of molded

LEFT **Renwal sewing machine, desk, chair, fireplace, and ashtray from the 1940s.**

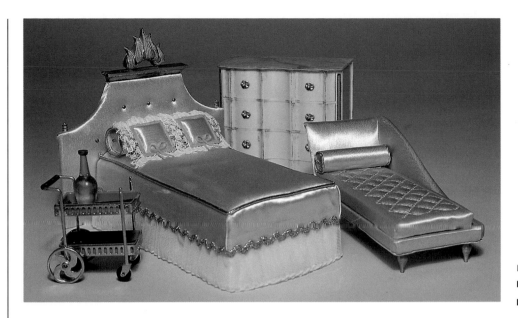

LEFT **A Petite Princess bedroom, in pink satin and plastic, made 1960.**

plastic furniture, and arranged for Petite Princess Fantasy Furniture to be made for it in Japan. It was 1:12 and very detailed, being hand-painted and upholstered in real fabrics. The furniture for the dining room, bedroom, and living room, cost $60, which was a very high price for that time. It did not sell, and was withdrawn after a year. Its characteristics include gilt mirrors and complex light fittings; there is an elaborate grand piano decorated with scenes in an 18th-century French style.

After this furniture was withdrawn, it was sold off by Ideal in boxed room settings under the name Princess Patti. Later still similar furniture was sold under the name Red Box, made in Hong Kong. This furniture, unwanted when new, was keenly collected at a later period.

Hong Kong became the center in the 1960s for the production of inexpensive, flexible plastic furniture, often on quite a small scale, and frequently sold in complete sets with a plastic house. Some of these sets were for many years marketed under the name Blue Box, but other furniture is simply marked "Made in Hong Kong."

BELOW **A Petite Princess grand piano, table, chairs and other items, made in 1960.**

The large American toy company Louis Marx, mentioned previously in connection with its tin furniture, also entered the plastic era with its Little Hostess range, which in Britain was marketed under the names Amanda Ann and Samantha Ann. Marx had a number of factories in the USA and abroad, but the company ran into difficulties and eventually closed down in the early 1970s. Its interests in Britain were subsequently taken over by Dunbee-Combex, which continued to market the Amanda Ann range.

Marx furniture was quite the most light-hearted and attractive of the postwar plastic series. Although having no great pretensions to be of interest to collectors, it mirrors the well-off if not very tasteful homes of that time. There is a grand piano to rival Petite Princess and a boudoir suite in acid pink, which is well realized. While this book has not attempted to deal with dolls, Marx includes a set of unjointed figures which also epitomize their period, including a boy wearing trousers quite tight and short enough for fashion.

A less common variant on Amanda Ann is the Walt Disney Dream House. This is a transparent perspex house in kit form, which came with Disney figures, a garden, and two cars, as well as a complete set of miniaturized Amanda Ann, the chairs being only 20 mm (¾ in) high. Daisy Duck has a Chippendale dining room with candelabra and a Chinese screen. A set in anything like a complete state is highly unusual to find.

Triang had continued to make its traditional dollhouses after the war, although with increasing use of metal and/or plastic. A factory for Spot On die-cast toys was set up in Belfast, Northern Ireland, and started to make dollhouse furniture in 1960. It was quite unusual in combining zinc cast-metal bases with plastic covering parts. Like all Triang toys, the furniture was very well made and detailed, being based on real commercial furniture. Thus the Kitchen was "Leisure," the bathroom was "Swanlyne," the radiogram was "Philips," and the refrigerator "Prestcold." This added greatly to a realistic effect.

The living room and bedroom furniture was originally mainly brown and black plastic, although for some unexplained reason Triang also marketed lounge, dining room and bedroom furniture in a basic wooden style. There was also a garden set, including a hammock, air mattress, and lounge chair, as well as many accessories such as a carpenter's bench and garden tools. The scale was 1:16.

In 1965 the furniture was relaunched as Jenny's Home, planned in association with *Homes and Gardens* magazine. A series of rectangular plastic rooms was provided to stack together as a house or a block of apartments, much in the style of local authority housing of the period. The furniture was recolored bright orange and turquoise. This range continued, with some alterations in 1969, until 1970, when production ceased. Lines/Triang was liquidated in 1971.

BELOW **An Amanda Ann boudoir in hard plastic. Louis Marx, America, 1960s.**

ABOVE **A Spot-On, Triang Jenny's Home, 1960s, lounge with** original carpet, in color scheme then fashionable!

Spot-On furniture has been increasingly collected, partly on its merits and partly because the Spot-On name appeals also to collectors of die-cast metal toys. Although often found boxed, the individual pieces are not marked, and not all pieces have the distinctive metal weighting.

Several other plastic ranges justify a brief mention, including the firm of Jean Hoefler of Fürth, near Nuremberg, Germany, which has made many inexpensive hard plastic sets marked Jean or Jeanette, and Mobystil of Burjasot Valencia, Spain, which has produced period-style ranges well-modeled in a wood brown finish.

An almost unclassifiable production was originally known as Spielwaren, and made by Rudolf Szalasi of West Germany, probably from the 1950s. This furniture imitates the baroque and rococo furnishings of German palaces, and was originally made of wood with applied composition decorations and silk or velvet upholstery, and a lot of gilt touches. It was widely available in the early 1970s. Later productions have some plastic parts.

Similar furniture was available in Britain from about the late 1950s to the early 1970s in a kit form. This was wholly plastic, with red nylon velvet upholstery, and was marketed by Scalecraft, a model manufacturer. Although sold for children, this furniture seems to have found a more appropriate habitat in the fantasy castles of adult miniaturists.

The children of the 1990s still have ranges of furniture by a few of the manufacturers mentioned in this chapter available to them, and in addition new models, such as Playmobil and Sylvanian Families, the latter designed for little animals rather than dolls to use. The dollhouse may sometimes go out of favor for a while, but it seems that so natural and charming a form of play will always be reintroduced in some new form.

Scale Miniatures

Miniatures have hardly ever ceased to have a place in the adult collecting world. At some periods the distinction between children's toys and miniatures has been blurred, as in the early 18th century, but usually they have been quite separate. Wholly adult was the 18th-century Princess Augusta Dorothea's miniature palace and town at Arnstadt, Germany, and so in more recent times were the collections of Mrs. Carlisle, who commissioned period rooms in the 1930s, and the dollhouse at Windsor Castle, designed for Queen Mary by the British architect Sir Edwin Lutyens. The furniture of these so far as possible is of high quality and in perfect scale, and the pleasure lies in the creation, rather than in any subsequent "play value."

The development of this hobby to cater for people of a wide variety of backgrounds, rather than a wealthy elite, took place in America in the postwar period. At this time the work of a number of miniature craftsmen became known through magazines, and enthusiasm grew both for making, furnishing, and decorating scale model houses at home, and for acquiring ready-built model houses and furniture from makers. The enthusiast could choose how much creative work she or he wished to do individually, and how much would be bought. This hobby became so popular that a thriving market developed for the components, including shops, books, magazines, catalogs, and fairs. Fairly rapidly, too, the production of less expensive ranges of scale-model furniture for this market started in factory rather than craft-based enterprises, especially in Taiwan. Nearly all of the models are in the form of more or less accurate reproductions of historic styles. It was only in the 1980s that this hobby really caught on in Britain, and it is not yet so popular in Europe.

So wide is the variety of goods available, from the frankly trivial to the unique masterpiece of miniature cabinet-making, that it is virtually impossible to make any fair selection in a book of this length. A few photographs are therefore included in the following chapter to give the reader an impression of what good work exists.

COLLECTING, REPAIRING, AND CONSERVING

CHAPTER **6**

ABOVE **Two bow-back Windsor chairs; contemporary miniatures.** (*Courtesy of The Singing Tree, London.*)

The previous chapters have of necessity been very selective, and some readers may well feel dissatisfied if a favorite object has been given only a brief mention. New collectors, on the other hand, may feel bewildered by such a catalog of types of furniture to collect, especially when they realize that dolls, curtains, carpets, and accessories are also needed to fill the house.

What to Collect

~

The question of what to collect is not one that anyone else can answer, although there are some guidelines. You should collect what appeals to you personally. Unless you are one of those people who simply enjoy the thrill of the chase and would be happy to collect car numbers, wait until something that you really like turns up, as it surely will. It is possible that your tastes may change eventually, but without some experimental purchases your knowledge and interest will not be able to develop.

It would not be wise to see dollhouse furniture in investment terms, although good quality antique pieces bought over the last 20 years would certainly have appreciated considerably. If you are concerned about expense, the advice is the same whatever collecting field you choose: buy only what seems to you to have real quality of workmanship and charm. Nevertheless, if you play too safe and collect only what is currently fashionable, you will pay highly for it, and may not be able to get your money back immediately if you need to.

Not all Waltershausen furniture, for instance, is of top quality, although the poorer pieces will still be expensive to buy. It is better, therefore, to forget fashion and buy interesting items of any period that you appreciate. At the present time, the most sought-after and expensive objects are the early German, British, and American tin; the gilt brass pieces, especially lighting equipment; Waltershausen; and the finest lithographed sets. German furniture from 1890 to 1930, which is often finely made and full of character, is under-appreciated. Also undervalued is the furniture made in a scale slightly larger than 1:12, as this requires a large dollhouse to set it off. This large furniture is often of fine quality, and will look wonderful in a room setting of the right scale.

LEFT **A longcase clock, with brass dial and walnut cross-banding; contemporary miniature. (Courtesy of The Singing Tree, London.)**

Condition is another matter which should be considered, although it is not quite as vital as in other toy collecting areas – for example, bisque dolls. Old toy furniture has often had a hard life, and may be broken or have bits missing or shabby upholstery. If all that is needed is careful cleaning and regluing, it is worth acquiring. If pieces are missing, especially turned parts, or if you cannot live with its shabby condition, then it might be best not to buy the piece. Restored pieces are not popular with collectors. With later furniture, especially plastic, perfect condition should be an essential requirement, as it is, of course, with new miniatures.

FAKES

Forgeries and fakes are not as common as in some other fields of collecting, although there are indications that, since certain types of furniture are now expensive, attempts are being made to reproduce them. Out-and-out forgeries are not such a problem at present as pieces that have been heavily restored, but where the vendor fails to draw attention to this fact. Tinplate pieces that have been repainted lose a lot of their value, and should be looked at carefully.

Many people will start with an empty dollhouse, and look for the right furniture to put in it. Some advice on buying a dollhouse that will be suitable to furnish is given in the first chapter. Most dollhouses that are not brand-new were designed to suit the toy furniture of the period in which they were made, and this is what will look best in them. Most of our own real houses are nowadays filled with an eclectic mixture of periods and styles, including antiques and reproductions. Some people furnish dollhouses in a similar way, and achieve a pleasing effect. In my view, however, this is never quite so successful in an old dollhouse as furnishing in period. To find out if you agree with this opinion, arrange to see one or two older houses furnished with their original pieces. The effect is a true feeling of the past, as if time had stood still in a locked room.

If it is impossible to find furniture of the exact period, as it will be for very old houses, aim for a mixture of items from a slightly later era. It is not wise to put modern reproductions in a genuine Georgian or Victorian house, however fine the craftsmanship. There are several reasons for this. First, the new wood will look different, and this will jar, even if "antiqued." Second, the modern pieces will usually be made to a precise 1:12 scale, and old houses are not always correctly proportioned to an exact scale; the contrast will be noticeable. Third, when we make something in the style of an earlier period, something of our own era inevitably clings to it, and this "smell" of the later period will soon become more apparent. This is one way in which fake works of art can be detected, for instance.

If you are still undecided how to start a collection of older pieces, one very enjoyable and probably not very expensive way is to buy a dollhouse from the period of your own childhood, and furnish it as you remember your parent's home. It will soon strike you how much things have changed in just a few decades, and how quickly our own era will slide into the past, and in turn amuse our children. If you wish to be ahead of the current fashion for nostalgia, you could start a

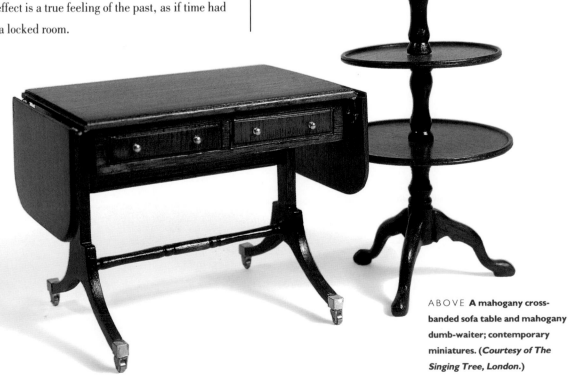

ABOVE **A mahogany cross-banded sofa table and mahogany dumb-waiter; contemporary miniatures. (*Courtesy of The Singing Tree, London.*)**

collection of furniture of the 1990s. You may well find, however, that the contemporary styles shown in interior decorating magazines are not yet being made for children.

Admirers of the superb craftsmanship of the modern miniaturist would be well advised to buy or have made a true miniature house to set off their collection. Alternatively, you could keep them, as was usual in Holland in the 18th century, in a handsome cabinet. In this field particularly, it would be a good idea for a beginner to buy the house before starting to collect the furniture, to ensure that the house and contents fit well together and suit each other's style. This may seem too obvious a point, but it is easy to buy pieces enthusiastically only to find they are wrong for the dollhouse you like.

How to Collect

As in any other collecting field, a little study before spending too much money is a very necessary precaution. Many people, even antique dealers, know virtually nothing about dollhouse furniture, and will describe it inaccurately, or overcharge for relatively common items.

Museums are a most important source of the necessary knowledge. Until very recently, in Britain at least, collections of toys in public museums were often not treated at all seriously. Curators would keep them in store, bringing out a selection at Christmas for the local children, often with hardly any information about the origin of the toys. This attitude, thanks to widespread coverage of toy collecting in the media, has begun to change.

However, dollhouses are still sometimes treated as no other antique object would be; original paintwork is "brightened-up" by applications of modern paint, and furniture is packed in boxes without a proper record of its original position in the rooms. One museum is said to have sawn off the roof of a particularly fine dollhouse in order to install unnecessary and anachronistic lighting.

For the collector, the most valuable museums are the specialized ones, whether municipal or private, where the houses and furniture are carefully displayed. Examples are the Bethnal Green Museum in London, the Washington Dolls' House and Toy Museum in America, and Vivien Greene's private museum in Oxford, England. In such places it is possible to see an old dollhouse with its original furniture still

ABOVE **An inlaid games table with lyre base and brass gallery; contemporary miniature.**

(*Courtesy of The Singing Tree, London.*)

in the positions chosen by its former owner. This is especially valuable to the furniture collector, as in former times furniture was not arranged as it is today. For example, paintings were often hung higher and more closely, and in certain periods chairs were ranged along the wall rather than standing in the center of the room.

A short list of museums and houses with fine collections that are open to the public is given on page 76, but there are many more. It might be worthwhile taking this book on visits, to help with identification.

Magazines and auction catalogs are among the best sources of up-to-date information on both new scale miniatures and old furniture. There are a number of magazines in America and Britain dealing with modern miniatures, with extensive advertising from craft businesses. The only one to cover old furniture equally extensively, so far as I am aware, is *International Dolls' House News*. Auction houses usually group dollhouses with dolls rather than toys, the latter mainly being metal trains and cars. Furniture is often unillustrated in the auction catalogs, unless it is of exceptional quality.

Membership of a local dollhouse club is another good

LITERATURE

Books are the other essential. Although a number can be regarded as classics, copies may be difficult to obtain except with the help of a library. These include Vivien Greene's two books, *English Dolls' Houses of the 18th and 19th Centuries* and *Family Dolls' Houses*; and Flora Gill Jacobs' *Dolls' Houses in America* and *Victorian Dolls' Houses and their Furnishings*. There are virtually no books dealing solely with old furniture, although it forms a part of most general accounts of dollhouses. Books about interior design and decoration in former times, furniture styles, and social history can be most informative. Some recommendations are given in the Bibliography.

For those interested in research, a number of old toy catalogs have been reproduced, and these can help to identify the origins of unusual pieces. The earlier catalogs were reproduced by wholesalers or agents and therefore do not include firms' names, but usually give the country of origin. Later catalogues were often issued by the manufacturers themselves. The catalogs of big stores can be misleading, as the country of origin of an item is rarely given, but they often give a wonderfully detailed impression of what was available at any particular time.

source of information, apart from offering companionship and arranging special visits to museums and private collections. There may also be opportunities to swop, buy, or sell items among club members.

Finding suitable pieces may involve exploring the possibilities of many different sources. For modern scale miniatures, details of specialized shops, mail order businesses and fairs can be found in the magazines. The hobby is so popular at present that new outlets are constantly appearing. As a result the buyer can and should be very discriminating. The specialized miniature fairs now held regularly are an excellent place to train the eye and compare the quality of the work. Fine workmanship cannot be cheap, as the maker must live, but in today's competitive market it is possible to find good value for money. Unfortunately, some exploitation of inexperienced buyers entering a growing market has occurred. The best safeguards against this are for the purchaser to have seen a wide range of products before choosing anything, and to understand the processes that

BELOW **A marble-topped console table with gilt metal base and a pair of gilt metal *torchères*;** contemporary miniatures. (*Courtesy of The Singing Tree, London.*)

RIGHT **An upholstered settee and armchair, covered in silk, with hand-painted cushions; contemporary miniatures.** (*Courtesy of The Singing Tree, London.*)

contribute to the making of a good piece of miniature furniture.

Old furniture is not easy to find. Specialized shops are limited in number but are extremely valuable, both for their stock and the knowledge of the owners, who are usually very happy to help people with a serious interest in the subject. Some dealers have regular stalls at weekly markets. Alternatively, there are specialized fairs; dollhouse furniture is mainly grouped with dolls, rather than toys, although some very large fairs cover both. Fairs advertised as dollhouse or miniature fairs may in fact have only new miniatures. Before traveling any distance, it would be sensible to contact the fair organizer to find out what is likely to be on sale.

Some stallholders at fairs may be very knowledgeable, others may know little about dollhouse furniture. This is even more true of ordinary antique fairs, where modern items may be overpriced out of ignorance, or occasionally a bargain may be found. For relatively recent items, especially those made in plastic, flea markets or garage sales, jumble sales and charity shops are good hunting grounds.

Auctions are the other major source for dollhouse collectors. All the major auction houses have specialized doll and toy sales, and in some countries there are specialized auctioneers. The viewing arrangements allow the collector to see and handle a wide variety of goods, adding considerably to knowledge without the need to spend any money. Buying at auction is not difficult, but it is not necessarily cheaper than buying from a dealer, especially if a number of people are bidding for a few good lots. It is essential to view carefully and decide on the maximum you wish to bid. Take the

auctioneers' descriptions with a pinch of salt, as only a few auction houses have a dollhouse specialist on their staff.

Restoring Furniture

~

Many pieces are in poor condition when bought. Like our own furniture when unloaded from a removal van, they will look shabby and unpromising outside their proper setting. It is, however, a mistake to rush into drastic renovation. The furniture will look much better set off by the carpets, wallpapers, and curtains of the dollhouse.

Detached legs and backs can be simply glued together, using the minimum quantity of white glue or woodworking adhesive according to the instructions given. Wipe off any surplus before it has hardened, because nothing looks worse than a thick shiny lump of glue over a join. Old glues, which are animal in origin, may simply deteriorate and fall apart; if this happens, scrape off every trace before regluing. If necessary, keep the glued pieces in place while setting with simple clamps or improvised methods using string, modeling clay, or masking tape.

Replacing a missing piece is more of an undertaking. Most collectors keep a stock of bits of old wood from broken furniture or old wooden boxes, because old wood must be used for a good repair. A piece of the right thickness can be cut with a fretsaw using a traced pattern. If there is access to a suitable lathe and a skilled turner, spindles and legs can be reproduced. Otherwise they can be carved by hand, or the chair can be put in a corner where the missing leg may not be noticed. A botched repair will be far more noticeable. It is virtually impossible for the amateur to reproduce the rosewood and other polished finishes of early German furniture perfectly. As this is the case, broken pieces of furniture can be satisfactorily mended only by cannibalizing other broken parts.

As far as upholstery is concerned, it is best to live with faded or worn covers, disguising them with cushions or a reclining doll. If absolutely necessary, chairs can be recovered in the finest silk or lawn, dyed at home to match the original.

Old fabrics including lace, silk and cotton are often very fragile, especially after 100 years at a window. If possible they should not be washed as it is difficult to be certain that they are color-fast and will not disintegrate. White cotton or linen, which may well stand gentle washing, should not be bleached, as the harsh blue-white of bleached material will not tone with old rooms.

If you are lucky enough to obtain wooden furniture with original painted finishes, do not be tempted to brighten the pieces up by repainting. Any unsightly bare areas could be discreetly filled in using thinned matt oil paints, and toned down with a coat of dirty matt varnish, then given a sheen with wax polish.

While this book does not deal with the renovation of dollhouses, it must be emphasized that the value of old houses and their interest to the collector depends very largely on their being in original condition, which means with original paintwork and papers inside and out. Houses that have been extensively renovated will lose a lot of their monetary value, a consideration now they are so expensive, and many collectors have spent countless hours removing with enormous patience the thoughtless "improvements" of the previous owners.

This does not, of course, mean that things should be neglected; the accurate replacement of missing pieces, careful cleaning, and a discreet use of wax polish will improve most dollhouses and furniture. The fashion for stripping and waxing painted or polished real furniture is now thankfully on the decline; this must never be inflicted on old dollhouse furniture.

The repair of metal requires different techniques, which cannot be covered in any detail here. Broken tinplate needs to be soldered together. The various types of soft cast-metal furniture can be glued together using epoxy glues. Missing

ABOVE **A working mantel clock, with brass inlay; contemporary miniature. (*Courtesy of The Singing Tree, London.*)**

ABOVE **A silver four-branch candelabrum; contemporary miniature. (*Courtesy of The Singing Tree, London.*)**

cast-metal parts can be replaced fairly successfully using casting methods, which involve making a mold using an existing part and casting the piece in white metal. Advice on materials and equipment can be obtained from model shops. It would be best to take any particularly valuable piece to a professional metal toy restorer, if you are able to obtain a recommendation from a friendly dealer, but make absolutely certain that you specify exactly the extent of the restoration which you require.

The repair of china and similar materials, except for valuable pieces, can be attempted at home using a product such as Milliput and/or epoxy glues.

Conservation

~

A hot, dry, centrally heated home is not a good environment for either old or new wood, which will tend to warp and split as it dries out. If possible, keep the house at a reasonable temperature. In the absence of humidifiers, experiment with keeping a small bowl of water in any accessible roof space. Sunlight, with its destructive rays of which we are now so much more aware, should be screened, especially where there are vulnerable old textiles.

Before your collection becomes too large, start a file or a database on which can be listed where, when and for how much each item was purchased, and any information obtained then or subsequently about the maker. Try to keep any boxes, folded flat if necessary. This is a counsel of perfection, but one that, in writing this book, the author very much wished she had invariably followed.

BIBLIOGRAPHY

Classic Books

~

Greene, Vivien, *English Dolls' Houses of the 18th and 19th Centuries*, Batsford, 1955; Bell and Hyman, London, 1979.

Greene, Vivien, *Family Dolls' Houses*, G. Bell and Sons, London, 1973.

Jacobs, Flora G., *Dolls' Houses in America*, Charles Scribner's Sons, New York, 1974.

Jacobs, Flora G., *A History of Dolls' Houses*, Charles Scribner's Sons, New York, Revised edition 1965.

Jacobs, Flora G., *Victorian Dolls Houses and their Furnishings*, Washington Dolls' House and Toy Museum, 1978.

Wilckens, Leonie., *Mansions in Miniature*, The Viking Press, New York, 1980 (mainly antique German).

General Books on Toys

~

Fawdry, K. & M., *Pollock's History of English Dolls and Toys*, E. Benn, London, 1979.

Flick, Pauline, *Discovering Toys & Toy Museums* (reprinted), Shire Publications, Aylesbury.

Fritzsch, K. & Bachmann, M., *An Illustrated History of Toys*, Abbey Library, 1966 (German toys).

White, Gwen, *Antique Toys and their Background*, Batsford, London, 1971.

White, Gwen, *Toys, Dolls, Automata: Marks & Labels*, Batsford, London, 1975.

General Books on Dollhouses

~

Earnshaw, Nora, *Collecting Dolls' Houses and Miniatures*, Collins, London, 1989.

King, C.E., *The Collector's History of Dolls' Houses*, Robert Hale, London, 1983.

Osborne, Marion, *Dolls' House A–Z*, from the author at 29 Attenborough Lane, Chilwell, Nottingham NG9 5JP, UK (compilation of advertisements, etc. from trade journals).

Dollhouse and Antique Furniture

~

Hennig, Claire, *So Lebten die Alten Puppen*, Wolfgang Kruger Verlag, Frankfurt, 1979 (picture book with German text).

Himmelheber, G., *Kleine Mobel*, Deutscher Kunst Verlag, München, 1979 (antique miniature furniture, German text).

Johnson, Audrey, *Furnishing Dolls' Houses*, Bell, London, 1972.

Schiffer, H.F. & P.B., *Miniature Antique Furniture*, Livingston Pub. Co., 1972 (American and English).

Doll's Rooms, Kitchens, etc.

~

Kunz J. & Schneiders, U., *Schone alte Puppenstuben*, Weingarten, Gmbh, 1986 (picture book with German text).

Reinelt, Sabine, *Puppenkuche und Puppenherd*, Weingarten, Gmbh, 1985 (picture book with German text).

Stille, Eva, *Doll Kitchens 1800–1980*, Schiffer Pub. Ltd., West Chester, Pennsylvania, 1988.

Metal Items

~

Cook, C. & Morris, E., *Fascinating Tin Toys for Girls*, pub. by authors, 1975.

De Voe, Shirley S., *The Art of the Tinsmith*, Schiffer Pub. Ltd., West Chester, Pennsylvania, 1981 (general book with references to toys).

Fawdry, Marguerite, *British Tin Toys*, New Cavendish Books, London, 1990.

Houart, V., *Miniature Silver Toys*, Alpine Fine Arts, New York, 1981.

Hrabvalek, Ernst, *Wiener Bronzen*, Laterna Magica, 1991 (Viennese bronzes including miniatures).

Pressland, David, *The Book of Penny Toys*, New Cavendish Books, London, 1991.

Firms

~

Manos, Susan, *Schoenhut Dolls and Toys*, Schroeder Pub. Co. Inc., Paducah, Kentucky, 1976.

Osborne, Marion, *Barton's Model Homes*, from the author, address as above.

Osborne, Marion, *Lines & Triang 1900–1971*, from the author, address as above.

Whitton, Blair, *Bliss Toys and Dollhouses*, Dover Pub. Inc., New York, 1979.

Catalogs

~

Ackerman, Evelyn, *Victorian Architectural Splendour*, Era Industries Inc., Culver City, California, 1980 (agent's catalog, of Moritz Gottschalk).

Bachmann, M., ed., *The Universal Toy Catalog of 1924–6*, New Cavendish Books, London, 1985. (German agent's catalog with much furniture, see text).

Baecker, C. & Vaterlein, C., *Vergessenes Blechspielzeug*, Verlag der Frankfurter & Buchhandling Michael Kohl, Frankfurt, 1982 (includes Rock & Graner, English text).

Bestelmeier, H., *Reprinted Catalog of 1803*, Edition Olms, Zurich, 1979.

Pieske, Christa, *Schones Spielzeug*, Idion Verlag, Munich, 1979 (Nuremberg catalogs of 1850s).

Paper Furniture

Jendrick, Barbara W., *Paper Dollhouses and Paper Dollhouse Furniture*, privately produced, 1975.

Whitton, Blair, *Paper Toys of the World*, Hobby House Press Inc., Cumberland, Maryland, 1986.

Dollhouse Dolls

Ackerman, Evelyn, *Dolls in Miniature*, Gold Horse Pub., Maryland, 1991.

Scale Miniature Houses

Hamilton, Caroline, *Decorative Dolls' Houses*, Weidenfeld & Nicolson, London, 1990.

The British Dolls' House Hobby Directory, L.D.F. Publications, 25 Priory Road, Kew, London, JW9 3DQ.

Ridley, Jessica, *The Decorated Dollshouse*, Macdonald, London, 1990.

Period Furniture and Interiors

(not miniature)

Cornforth, J., *English Interiors, 1790–1848*, Barrie & Jenkins, London, 1989.

Gere, Charlotte, *19th-Century Decoration*, Weidenfeld & Nicolson, London, 1989.

Lancaster, O., *Homes Sweet Homes*, John Murray, London, 1939.

Lasdun, Susan, *Victorians at Home*, Weidenfeld & Nicolson, London, 1981.

Thornton, P., *Authentic Decor, 1620–1920*, Weidenfeld & Nicolson, London, 1984.

Yarwood, Doreen, *The English Home*, Batsford, London, 1979.

Magazines

International Dolls' House News, P.O. Box 79, Southampton SO9 7EZ, UK.

Dolls' House World, Ashdown Publishing Ltd, Shelley House, 104 High Street, Steyning, W. Sussex BN4 3RD, UK.

Nutshell News, Kalmbach Miniatures Inc., 21027 Crossroads Circle, P.O. Box 1612, Waukesha, WI 53187, USA.

SOME AUCTION HOUSES WITH SPECIALIZED SALES

Britain

Bonhams, Chelsea.
Christie's, South Kensington and Scotland.
Philips, London, Sherborne, and Leeds.
Sotheby's, London and Billingshurst.

France

Chartres, Galérie de Chartres.

Switzerland

Peter Inieichen, Zurich.

United States

Theriault's, Maryland.

USEFUL ADDRESSES

Britain

Museum of Childhood, Bethnal Green.
Pollock's Toy Museum, London.
The Rotunda, Iffley, Oxford.
The Precinct Toy Collection, Sandwich.
Ribchester Museum of Childhood, Lancashire.
Wallington House (National Trust), Northumberland.

Denmark

Legoland, Billund.

France

Musée du Jouet, Poissy.
Musée des Arts Decoratifs, Paris.

Germany

Nuremberg Toy Museum.
Germanische Nationalmuseum, Nuremberg.
Arnstadt Castle, Thüringia.
Heimat Museum, Überlingen.

The Netherlands

Rijks Museum, Amsterdam.
Centraal Museum, Utrecht.
Gemeente Museum, The Hague.
Stedelijk Museum, Haarlem.
Frans Hals Museum, Haarlem.

Sweden

Nordiska Museet, Stockholm.

United States

Angel's Attic, Santa Monica, CA.
Atlanta Toy Museum, Atlanta, GA.
Toy and Miniature Museum, Kansas City, MI.
Margaret Woodbury Strong Museum, Rochester, NY.
Washington Dolls' House and Toy Museum, Washington D.C.

MAKERS AND MANUFACTURERS

Agents, shops, and wholesalers have been excluded unless their names have become attached to a type of furniture whose maker is unknown. In some cases it is not known if the toys were doll or dollhouse size. References to the Universal Toy Catalog are shown as UTC, followed by code number and pages. This list does not in any way pretend to be comprehensive as the subject is in many areas largely unresearched.

Austria

Haller, J.: c.1851. Vienna. Exhibited miniature furniture at Crystal Palace.
Wallach & Co.: 1920s. Vienna. Furniture.

Britain

Amersham Works Ltd.: 1940s. Union Street, London. Proprietor: Leon Rees. Dollhouse firm, advertised British-made furniture.
Avery W. & Sons: 1860s. Redditch. Needlecases.
Barrett, A. & Sons (Toys) Ltd.: 1945–83, London. Metal and plastic accessories.
Barthel Bros. & Warren: 1921. Aldermanbury, London. Wooden furniture.
Barton, A. & Co. (Toys) Ltd.: 1945–84. London. Wooden and plastic furniture. Tradename "Caroline's Home."
Bestikion Toys Ltd.: 1916–20s. Judd Street, London. Papier mâché food and tableware.
Bigco (The British Indoor Games Co. Ltd.): 1915. London. Cardboard furniture.
W. Britain, Messrs & Sons: 1890–present. Hornsey, London. Cast accessories.
British Xylonite Co. Ltd.: c.1937. Hale End, London. Bakelite furniture. Tradename Bex.
Bubb, John: 1809–37. Long Lane, Bermondsey, London. Mahogany furniture.

Cartwright, A. S., Ltd.: 1880–1940s. Birmingham. Tradename Holdfast. Tinplate sets and Gwenda sets.
Charbens & Co. Ltd.: 1929–80. Hornsey, London. Metal toys. Small-scale, cast-metal furniture in the 1930s.
Cowan de Groot & Co.: 1919–60. Bunhill Row, London. Wholesaler. Tradename Codeg used, inter alia, for mottled plastic furniture in the 1950s.
Crescent Toy Co. Ltd.: 1922–80. Kingsland Road, London, and Wales. Small-scale, cast metal in the 1950s.
Dol-Toi Products (Stamford) Ltd.: 1944–78. Wooden furniture.
Elgin Ltd.: 1919–26. Enfield. Wooden furniture. Mark "Elgin/Enfield" impressed.
Erhardt, S. & Sons: see Graham Bros.
Evans & Cartwright: c.1800–80. Dudley Road, Wolverhampton. Tinplate furniture. Mark: "Evans & Cartwright" impressed (very small).
Graham Bros. (formerly Erhardt, S. & Sons): 1887–1950s. London. Wholesalers, including Japanese porcelain, wood, cast metal. Tradename: Fairylite.
Handicrafts Ltd.: 1907–30s. Kentish Town, London. Fretwork patterns and kits.
Hill, John & Co.: 1906–56. Islington, London. Tradename: Johilco. Cast metal, including tea and kitchen sets; similar to Britains.
Hobbies Ltd.: 1895–1970. Dereham, Norfolk. Fretwork patterns and kits.
Holladay, A. J. & Co. Ltd.: 1918 onwards. London. Wholesaler. Metal and china items. Tradename "Givjoy."
Homeland Toys: 1914–c.1919. Liverpool. Wooden furniture, kitchens, houses.
Hopkins Bros.: 1880–c.1920. Victoria Tin Toys Works, London. Tinplate furniture.
Jacqueline: 1940s. British-made, cast metal, sold by B.S. (Mgf. & Dist.) Co.; maker unknown.
Joseph, J.: c.1917. Clapham, London. Fabric-covered wood furniture.
Kay (Sports & Games) Ltd.: 1935–c.1948. London. Plastic and tinplate furniture.

Kaybot Novelties: 1950s. London. Toy food, bottles, packets, etc.
Kew's Ltd.: c.1934. Brockley, London. Cast-metal furniture. Tradename Modlets.
Kiddicraft Ltd.: 1960s. Kenley, Surrey. Toy food, bottles, tins, etc.
Kleemann O. & M., Ltd.: 1902 to present. Plastic furniture during 1940s–50s.
Kyteland Mfg. Co.: c.1920. Ludgate Circus, London. Wooden furniture.
Lehman, E. & Co.: 1920s–50s. London. Wooden furniture. Tradename "Pit a Pat."
Lines Bros Ltd.: 1919–71. London, Merton, Wales. Dollhouses, wooden and plastic furniture. Tradenames Triangtois, Triang, Jenny's Home, Spot-On.
Lord Roberts' Memorial Workshops: 1899–1920s. Fulham Road, London. Wooden furniture.
Meccano Ltd.: 1901–81. Binns Road, Liverpool. Tradename Dinky Toys. Cast-metal Dolly Varden furniture.
Parkstone Toy Factory: 1915. Dorset. Wooden furniture and houses.
Peacock & Co. Ltd.: 1853–c.1930. London. Wooden furniture, shops, etc.
Reka Ltd.: 1909–30s. London. Cast-metal accessories.
Rellaw: 1940s onwards. Wooden furniture.
Taylor, F. G. & Sons Ltd.: 1945–80. London. Cast-metal and plastic accessories.
Taylor & Barrett: 1920–41. London. Cast-metal accessories.
Tiny Toys: c.1932. St John Street, London. Wooden and cast metal in two scales.
Wells-Brimtoy (various names): 1914 to present. Walthamstow (1950s). Tradename Welsotoys. Made My Dolly's Kitchen (c.1955). Earlier made kitchen stoves under Brimtoy Brand.
Westacre Village: 1930s. Norfolk. Handmade lacquered wooden pieces.
Whitehouse, G. & Co. (Birmingham) Ltd.: 1940s. Tubular tin-plate furniture.

Denmark

~

Hanse: 1960s. Modern wooden furniture.

Finland

~

Nordensvan, M. Kuopio: 1890s. Fine quality wooden furniture.

France

~

Simon & Rivollet: 1890s–1920s. Paris. Cast-metal penny toys. Mark: "S.R."

Germany

~

Auerbach, Richard: 1902–c.1926. Eppendorf, Saxony. Furniture, singly or boxed.

Baur, Gebrüder: c.1926. Biberach-an-der-Riss, Baden-Württemberg. Articles for toy shops and kitchens.

Bäselsöder, J.A.: 1850s–1909. Nuremberg. Tinplate toys, including furniture.

Beier, Oskar: c.1926. Waldkirchen, Zschopenthal, Saxony. Wooden toys, including houses, rooms, furniture (Erzgebirge Miniatures).

Beyermann & Co.: 1920s. Haida, Dresden. Miniature glassware, plain and decorated.

Bochmann, Carl: 1926 onwards. Dresden N12, Saxony. Metal toys including stoves, washstands, and bathroom sets.

Börner, Adolf: 1869–c.1926. Zeitz, Saxony. Metal toys, including beds, washstands.

Bing-Werke, Gebrüder Bing A.G.: 1860s–1925. Nuremberg. Metal toys including kitchens and kitchen utensils.

Blumhardt, Henry: 1851–c.1885. Stuttgart. Tinplate houses, upholstered furniture, painted and gilt.

Brandt, Carl Jr: c.1850–1926 onwards. Gössnitz, Saxony. Furniture, single or in sets, large manufacture. Villa construction set. UTC, 39, 145–7.

Dahnert, Linus: c.1924. Wünschendorf, Saxony. White lacquered furniture.

Dieterich, C. F.: 1842–c.1926. Rosenstrasse, Ludwigsberg, Württemberg. Stoves, kitchen equipment in tin, copper, aluminum. Toy swimming pools.

Distler, Johann. 1900–30s. Nuremberg. Penny toys. Mark "J.D."

Dorst, Julius: 1865–c.1926. Sonneberg, Thuringia. Large firm producing wood and composition toys, including dollhouses and, possibly, furniture.

Eppendorfer & Knacke: c.1921. Eppendorf, Saxony. Furniture.

Fischer, Georg: 1903–30s. Nuremberg. Penny toys. Mark "G.F."

Fischer, Gustav: 1880–1926 onwards. Zöblitz, Saxony. Tinplate stoves, baths, and coffee mills.

Fischer, F. & R. A. G.: 1875–c.1926 onwards. Göppingen, Württemberg. Tinplate cooking stoves.

Gerlach, F. W.: 1850–1939. Naumberg, Thuringia. Pewter toys, dollhouse accessories, doll's rooms and kitchens.

Gottschalk, Moritz: 1865–1939. Marienberg, Saxony. Major manufacturer of dollhouses; furniture. UTC 7, 139–41.

Gotz, Chr. & Sohn: 1930 onwards, Fürth, Bavaria. Tinplate toys, washstands, etc.

Gross, Carl: 1842–c.1926. Esslingen A.N. Large wooden toys, including toy shops and contents.

Hacker, Christian: 1870s–1914. Nuremberg. Dollhouses, shops with fittings, and furnished rooms.

Hahnel, Oskar: 1874–c.1924. Grünhainichen, Saxony. Furniture, houses, kitchens, rooms.

Hennig, Walter: c.1924 onwards. "Ola" Spielwaren Fabrik, Borstendorf, Saxony. Furniture.

Hennig, Bodo: 1980s–90s. Wildpoldsried. Furniture.

Hubsch, Paul: 1920s. Seiffen, Saxony. Furniture. *See also* Ulrich & Hoffman.

Hunger, Paul. 1892–c.1926. Eppendorf, Saxony. Furniture, especially in cartons.

Hunger, L.: 1930s. Eppendorf, Saxony. Furniture.

Kindler & Briel: 1865–present. Böblingen, Baden-Württemburg. Wood and metal toys, shops, furniture, etc. UTC 17, 110–117.

Kohnstam, Moses: 1890s–c.1930. Olbernhau Saxony. Wholesaler, distributed from this branch dollhouses and furniture under Tradename "MOKO."

Knosp & Backe: c.1851. Stuttgart. Pasteboard furnished doll's rooms.

Krause, Theodore. 1853–c.1924. Saxony. Metal furniture, baths, etc.

Kreher, Clemens: c.1926. Marienberg, Saxony. Metal stoves and kitchen equipment, etc.

Kühnrich, Georg: 1900–c.1926. Waldheim, Saxony. Successor to Gebrüder Tamm, acquired Rock & Graner equipment. Metal and papier mâché toys, doll's rooms, and furniture.

Leonhardt, Paul: 1894–c.1926. Eppendorf, Saxony. Furniture, doll's rooms, shops. UTC 50, 224i–ix.

Linke, Oskar: Heidersdorf, Saxony. Wooden toys, furniture.

Lutz, Ludwig: 1846–91. Ellwangen, Württemberg. Tinplate enameled furniture.

Märklin, Gebrüder. Göppingen, Württemberg: Metal toys, including furniture.

Meier, Johann Phillip: 1879–1934. Nuremberg. Penny toys.

Oehme, Carl Heinrich: 1787–c.1946. Waldkirchen, Saxony. Erzgebirge toys, furniture, kitchens. This family firm of agents, which produced a fine sample book in 1850, collected products from small firms in the area.

Paris, Gebrüder: c.1926. Oberkoditz, Thuringia. Miniature porcelain.

Reil, Blechschmidt & Muller: 1900s–20s. Brandenburg. Tinplate toys including toy furnished rooms. "ORO."

Richter & Wittich: 1891–c.1926. Eppendorf, Saxony. Furniture, forts, etc.

Rock & Graner: 1825–c.1904. Biberach, Württemberg. Tinplate furniture, painted and upholstered.

Schubert, E. E.: 1874–c.1926. Grünhainichen, Saxony. Wooden toys, doll's rooms, shops, and kitchens.

Schneegas, Gebrüder: 1830s–1940s. Waltershausen, Thuringia. Furniture, single and in cartons, schools.

Schweitzer, Babette: 1790s to present. Diessen-am-Ammersee. Soft pewter cast furniture, filigree, etc.

Sohlke, G.: c.1851. Berlin. Cast-pewter dinner and tea services.

Striebel, G.: 1830s–50. Biberach, Württemberg. Enameled tinplate kitchen utensils.

Szalasi: 1950s 80s. Bavaria. Wood and composition furniture. Tradename Spielwaren.

Ulbricht, Bruno: 1920s. Nuremberg, Bavaria. Metal toys, including furniture and kitchen items.

Ulmer Holz & Spielwaren-Werkstätten, E. Hillebrands Erben K. G.: c.1926. Ulm-an-der-Donau. Furniture, dollhouses and rooms, toys gardens. UTC 119, 310–11.

Ulrich & Hoffman: 1920s–60s. Seiffen, Saxony. "Hubsch" furniture, kitchens.

Vero: 1960s–80s. Olbernhau, Saxony. Wooden furniture, in room boxes, etc.

Wachtler, August: c.1926. Fürth, Bavaria. Tin and aluminum coffee sets, kitchen ware.

Wagner, Heinrich: 1920s. Grünhainichen, Saxony. Wooden furniture.

Wittich, Kemmel & Co.: 1840s. Geislingen, Ivory miniature furniture.

Italy

INGAP (Industria Nazionale Giocattoli Automatici Padua): 1919 to present. Tin furniture.

Japan

K.K.: 1920s–30s. Wooden furniture.

New Zealand

Fun Ho!: 1939–87. New Plymouth. Die-cast metal furniture made in 1940s.

Poland

Gleiwitz Iron Foundry: 1840s. Pincushions in form of chairs, sofas, etc.

Herz & Erlich: 1890s. Breslau. Metal kitchen furniture, etc.

Roithner, Hugo: 1871–c.1926. Schweidnitz. Wooden furniture, rooms.

Spain

Rico, Ibi: 1920 to present. Lithographed tinplate furniture.

Sri Lanka

Royden: 1970s–80s. Traditional wooden furniture.

Sweden

Brio, Osby: 1884 to present. Wooden toys; made plastic furniture in 1970s–80s.

Lundby, Lerum. 1950s to present. Wooden and plastic furniture.

Gemla Leksaksfabriks (Westerdahl's Fabrik): 1866–c.1911. Furniture (also rocking horses).

U.S.A

Althof, Bergmann & Co: c.1867. New York. Tin furniture. Trademark ABC.

Arcade Mfg. Co.: 1920s–30s. Freeport, Illinois. Cast-iron furniture.

American Art Toymakers: c.1916. Chicago. Enameled steel furniture.

Bliss, R. Manufacturing Co.: 1832–1914. Pawtucket (Taken over by Mason & Parker, cont. to 1935). Lithographed paper on wood.

Buck, Geo. H.: c.1914. Brooklyn, N.Y. Metal beds, etc.

Child's Welfare Co.: c.1916. Chicago. Wooden furniture.

Cooke, Adrian, Metallic Works: 1900s. Chicago. Cast aluminum furniture. Tradename "Fairy."

Dowst Mfg. Co.: 1870s–1963. Chicago. Cast-metal furniture. Tradename Tootsietoy.

Ellis, Britton, & Eaton: 1860s–70s. Vermont. Tin and iron furniture.

Francis, Field, & Francis: 1840s–50s. Philadelphia. Tin furniture.

Grandmother Stover's Miniatures: c.1940. Metal accessories.

Ideal Novelty & Toy Co.: 1940s–60s. Plastic furniture. Tradenames Petite Princess, Princess Patti.

Harco: 1930s. Wooden furniture.

Hull & Stafford: 1860s–1880s. Clinton, Connecticut. Tin furniture.

Kilgore: 1920s–30s. Westerville, Ohio. Cast-iron furniture.

Marx, Louis, & Co.: 1920s–67. USA. Tin and plastic furniture. Tradename "Newlyweds."

Mattel Inc.: Hawthorne, California. Postwar die-casts. Tradename The Littles.

Miniature Toy Co.: 1940–50s. Chicago. Metal accessories. Tradename Mintoy.

Plastic Toy & Novelty Corporation: 1945–57. Brooklyn. Hard plastic furniture. Tradename Plasco.

Peter F. Pia: 1840s–1900s. New York. Cast white metal furniture.

Renwal: 1940s–60s. Plastic furniture.

Schoenhut, A. & Co.: 1872–1934. Philadelphia. Wooden furniture.

Stevens & Brown: c.1868. Connecticut. Formed by merger of Stevens and G. Brown. Tin and iron furniture.

Strombecker Co.: 1920s–50s. Moline, Illinois. Wooden furniture.

Tynietoy: 1920–50. Providence, Rhode Island. Wooden furniture.

Tower Toy Guild: 1860–1914. Hingham, Massachusetts. Wooden furniture.

Wilder Mfg. Co.: c.1914. St. Louis. Wooden furniture, room settings.

INDEX